Colin Wilson:
Philosopher of Optimism

Colin Wilson:
Philosopher of Optimism

Brad Spurgeon

MICHAEL BUTTERWORTH

First published in Great Britain in 2006 by
Michael Butterworth

2 4 6 8 10 9 7 5 3 1

Michael Butterworth
michael-butterworth@ntlworld.com

A CIP catalogue record for this book is
available from the British Library

ISBN 0-9552672-0-X
ISBN 978-0-9552672-0-8

Printed and bound by CPI Antony Rowe Ltd, Eastbourne

Jacket design by Fine'n'Dandy
www.studio-dust-com

Typography by Sara Inkster

Author's Dedication

For my wife Nathalie,
and my children Paul and Emily
– whose patience has made my writing possible

Acknowledgements

'Article for The Big Idea' originally appeared in
Adbusters 2006

'Introduction to Paul Hougham's Gaia Atlas of Mind, Body
and Spirit' originally appeared in the Gaia Atlas of Mind,
Body and Spirit by Paul Hougham, Gaia 2006

'Phenomenology as a Mystical Discipline' originally
appeared in Philosophy Now, 2006

Photographs courtesy of the Wilson family
i – At Gorran Haven by Alex Bourdelon
ii – Joy Wilson
viii, xvi and 40 – Dan Farson, for Harper's Bazaar 1956

Special thanks to Joy Wilson

Contents

Philosopher of Optimism Endures Negative Deluge*

Any intellectual who divides opinion as much as Colin Wilson has for almost fifty years must be onto something, even if it is only whether humans should be pessimistic or optimistic.

Wilson, who will turn seventy-five in June 2006, describes in the first chapter of his recently published autobiography, *Dreaming to Some Purpose*, how he made his own choice. The son of working-class parents from Leicester – his father was in the boot and shoe trade – he was forced to quit school and go to work at sixteen, even though his ambition was to become 'Einstein's successor' After a stint in a wool factory, he found a job as a laboratory assistant, but he was still in despair and decided to kill himself.

---

*A slightly expanded version of an article by Brad Spurgeon that origi-nally appeared in the International Herald Tribune and The New York Times, August 17th 2005

On the verge of swallowing hydrocyanic acid, he had an insight: there were two Colin Wilsons, one an idiotic, self-pitying teenager and the other a thinking man, his real self.

The idiot, he realised, would kill them both.

"In that moment," he wrote, "I glimpsed the marvelous, immense richness of reality, extending to distant horizons."

Achieving such moments of optimistic insight has been his goal and subject matter ever since, through more than a hundred books, from his first success, *The Outsider*, published in 1956, when he was declared a major existentialist thinker at twenty-four, to the autobiography.

In an interview at his home of nearly fifty years on the Cornish coast, Wilson was as optimistic as ever, even though his autobiography and his life's work have come under strong attack in some quarters.

"What I wanted to do was to try to create a philosophy upon a completely new foundation," he said, sitting in his living room along with a parrot, two dogs and part of his collection of thirty thousand books and as many records.

"Whereas in the past optimism had been regarded as rather shallow – because 'oh well, it's just your temperament, you happen to be just a cheerful sort of person' – what I wanted to do was to establish that in fact it is the pessimists who are allowing all kinds of false assumptions to creep into their work."

He includes in that category writers like Hemingway and philosophers like Sartre. In books on sex, crime, psychology and the occult, and in more than a dozen novels, Wilson has explored how pessimism can rob ordinary people of their powers.

"If you asked me what is the basis of all my work," he said, "it's the feeling there's something basically wrong with human beings. Human beings are like grandfather clocks driven by watch springs. Our powers appear to be taken away from us by something."

The critics, particularly in Britain, have alternately called him a genius and a fool. His autobiography, when it appeared in 2004, received mixed reviews. Though lauded by some, the attacks on it and Wilson have been as virulent as those he provoked in the 1950s after he became a popular culture icon with the publication of *The Outsider*.

That book dealt with alienation in thinkers, artists and men of action like TE Lawrence, van Gogh, Camus and Nietzsche, and caught the mood of the age. Critics, including Cyril Connolly and Philip Toynbee, hailed Wilson as a British version of the French existentialists.

His fans ranged from Muammar el-Qaddafi to Groucho Marx, who asked his British publisher to send a copy of his own autobiography to three people in Britain: Winston Churchill, Somerset Maugham and Colin Wilson.

The Outsider was translated into dozens of languages and sold millions of copies. It has never been out of print.

The Times of London called Wilson and John Osborne – another young working-class writer, whose play *Look Back in Anger* opened about the same time *The Outsider* was published – 'angry young men'. That name was passed on to others of their generation, including Kingsley Amis, Alan Sillitoe and even Doris Lessing.

But fame brought its own problems for Wilson. His sometimes tumultuous early personal life became fodder for gossip columnists. He was still married to his first wife while living with his future second wife, Joy. His publisher, Victor Gollancz, urged him to leave the spotlight, and he and Joy moved to Cornwall.

But the publicity had done its damage. His second book,

Religion and the Rebel, was panned and his career looked dead.

Wilson said the episode had actually saved him as a writer, however.

"Too much success gets you resting on your laurels and creates a kind of quicksand that you can't get out of," he said. "So I was relieved to get out of London."

He said his books were probably heading for condemnation in Britain anyway. "I'm basically a writer of ideas, and the English aren't interested in ideas," he said. "The English, I'm afraid, are totally brainless. If you're a writer of ideas like Sartre or Foucault or Derrida, then most people in France at least know your name, whereas here in England, their equivalent in the world of philosophy wouldn't be known."

He never lost belief in the importance of what he was saying: the importance of the task of learning to harness our powers, and throw off the cultural pessimism that turned the twentieth century into what he called 'the age of defeat'.

"Sartre's 'man is a useless passion,' and Camus's claim that life is absurd and meaningless, basically meant that philosophy itself had turned negative and impotent," he said. "My basic insight was that there was a fallacy in the existentialism of Sartre, Camus, Heidegger and so on. The basic fallacy lay in their failure to understand the actual foundation of the problem."

That foundation, he said, is that human perception is intentional. What this means is that in order to see anything you have to direct attention at it like a whaler throwing a harpoon. If you look at your watch without this intentionality, you don't notice the time, and have to look again.

Yet we do most of our perceiving without realising that it is intentional. In other words, there is a kind of hidden 'you' behind your everyday self. And it is this 'hidden you' that is the cause for optimism, because if you recognise it and make use of it, it can change your life.

Pessimists are people who have infected their 'hidden you' with self-pity and negativity. They paint their world black without realising what they are doing. Becoming aware of the powers of the 'hidden you' is the first step in self-change.

Wilson has spent much of his life researching how to achieve those moments of well-being that bring insight into the 'hidden you', the self behind the self. This happens whenever we get one of those odd flashes of happiness, which Chesteron called 'absurd good news', and what the American psychologist Abraham Maslow called 'peak experiences'.

Those moments can come spontaneously, as when Proust tasted a biscuit dipped in tea, or through effort, concentration or focus, and refusing to lose one's vital energies through pessimism.

"What it means basically is that you're able to focus until you suddenly experience that sense that everything is good," Wilson said. "We go around leaking energy in the same way that someone who has slashed their wrists would go around leaking blood.

"Once you can actually get over that and recognise that this is not necessary, suddenly you begin to see the possibility of achieving a state of mind, a kind of steady focus, which means that you see things as extremely good."

If harnessed by everyone, this could lead to the next step in human evolution, a kind of Superman.

"The problem with human beings so far is that they are met with so many setbacks that they are quite easily defeatable, particularly in the modern age when they've got too separated from their roots," he said.

Following publication of his autobiography, he has been forced to test his own powers in this area.

"When I was pretty sure that the autobiography was going to be a great success, and when it, on the contrary, got viciously attacked," Wilson said, "well, I know I'm not wrong. Obviously the times are out of joint.

"I knew I wasn't mistaken in thinking it my best book. In the first chapter, I tell a story of lecturing on the same platform as RD Laing and the poet David Gascoyne. Both had had nervous breakdowns at some time. And it became obvious that both were somehow outraged that I didn't share their feeling that life is an awful trap. So they ganged up and attacked me. I suspect many of the attacks on the book sprang from the same attitude."

Though *Dreaming to Some Purpose* was warmly received in The Independent on Sunday and The Spectator and was praised by the novelist Philip Pullman, the autobiography – and Wilson – received a barrage of negative profiles and reviews in The Sunday Times and The Observer. One interviewer, known for her acid profiles, concentrated on Wilson's admission that he had a lifelong fetish for women's panties, but avoided writing about his ideas.

As a measure of the passions that Wilson provokes, Robert Meadley, a highly individual essayist, wrote *The Odyssey of a Dogged Optimist**, a 188-page book defending him.

"If you think a man's a fool and his books are a waste of time, how long does it take to say so?" Meadley wrote, questioning the space the newspapers gave to the attacks.

Part of Meadley's conclusion is that the British intellectual establishment still felt threatened by Wilson, a self-educated outsider from the working class.

*The Odyssey of a Dogged Optimist, Savoy Books 2004. Free download www.savoy.abel.co.uk

"One of my main problems as far as the public is concerned is that I've always been interested in too many things," Wilson said. "Apart from existential philosophy, which is the subject of the seven books of the 'Outsider' cycle, I've written extensively on mysticism, psychology, criminology, the paranormal, history, ancient civilisations, music, even a book on wine. If they can't typecast you, then I'm afraid you tend not to be understood at all."

Introduction

In 1984 while writing a novel that began taking on a supernatural theme, I decided I'd do well to learn something about the supernatural, since it was a subject I knew nothing about. It was my father, a science journalist, who directed me to Colin Wilson's book, *The Occult*, which he said was a well-respected work on such a difficult subject.

Although I knew of Wilson as the author of *The Outsider*, I had never read any of his books, though I had always been meaning to. I enjoyed *The Occult* so much that I immediately bought his other occult books, and with my interest in crime writing, I was soon reading his crime books. I finally made my way to *The Outsider*, and other books in the 'Outsider' cycle, and they were the ones I enjoyed the most.

It was ironic that I had started with the occult and crime books, since my main interests in reading are more literary and philosophical. On the other hand, Wilson is the kind of writer who infuses all of his books with certain common themes, and as a result, it really is possible to start just about anywhere, and work one's way around.

One of the reasons I enjoy his writing so much, is his common sense approach to the world while at the same time he is someone whose mind is open to anything. Reading Wilson makes me feel optimistic about life in general, and constantly reminds me of why it is good to live.

He is also the kind of writer who develops such a close rapport with his readers that one feels one knows him personally through his writing. That is why I had no qualms about writing a letter to him immediately in 1984 about something to do with that supernatural novel. It turned out to be the beginning of a correspondence of perhaps half a dozen letters over a ten-year period. He kindly and politely responded to every letter I sent him with interesting, educational responses. I know I had little to offer to him, but I enjoyed the intellectual exchange immensely. Even so, I eventually ran out of reasons to write, and after reading so many of his books, I moved on to other things.

But when last year I noticed that he had recently published his autobiography, *Dreaming to Some Purpose*, I ordered it from an English-language bookstore in Paris. Having read so many of his books, I was very curious to learn about his life. It was an even more wondrous read than I had expected, describing not only his own rise to fame, but his meetings and impressions of so many of the post-war literary icons that I had admired – or at least heard of.

Literary autobiography being one of my favourite genres, I thought that it was a good moment to write to Wilson again just to tell him how much I had enjoyed the book.

"It's right up there on my favourites list with *Memories, Dreams, Reflections* by Jung; Ford Madox Ford's autobiographical writings; Hemingway's *A Moveable Feast; Being Geniuses Together* by Robert McAlmon and Kay Boyle; Charlie Chaplin's autobiography; Gertrude Stein's *Autobiography of Alice B Toklas;* and Powys' autobiography," I wrote. [*I forgot one that would come up later in the interview, his friend Stephen Spender's* World Within World]

I told him that I hoped that I could meet him soon, and perhaps do a story about him for the International Herald Tribune, where I work. I wanted to peg the story to both the publication of the autobiography and the upcoming 50th anniversary of the publication of *The Outsider.*

He wrote me back by email – our previous correspondence had always been by surface mail, but times had changed – and told me he was delighted to have heard from me, particularly to hear how much I liked the autobiography. It turned out, he said, that it had been received with "coolness and hostility", by some of the British newspapers.

Before I looked up the details on that, I pitched the idea at the IHT, telling my editor that I would be travelling to England in the summer anyway, and would drop by his place to interview him. The editor accepted the idea with the proviso, "As long as he has something interesting to say." I was told that sometimes writers write well, but are not very interesting people to speak to, and have little of interest to say for an article.

So it was that I set out on my journey in July by air from Paris to Bristol and from there by rental car to Cornwall, stopping halfway for a night in a hotel along the motorway near Exeter, before driving the rest of the trek to his place in Gorran Haven the next morning. The whole time I feared that if Wilson had "nothing to say", I would have wasted my time – and his time – except for the thrill of meeting one of my favourite writers.

As it turned out, I was relieved to discover that not only did this writer have something interesting to say, but also that he was almost tireless in doing so, taking great pleasure in talking. He had, in fact, so much to say that I ended up with a newspaper story that proved so successful that it was not only used in the IHT, but also picked up for same-day publication in The New York Times, where it received half a page of display. It then went on to be copied and quoted on web sites and blogs around the world by people who found Wilson's words supremely relevant in today's pessimistic times.

Before writing the article, I did not have the time to transcribe the full interview. But I returned to that at the end of the year, and by the time I finished the transcription, I realised that I had twenty thousand words of Wilson speaking. I had more than just a newspaper story. I had a book.

Provided, of course, that I could find a publisher. One of the results of doing the story was my discovery of Robert Meadley and the small publisher based in Manchester, called Savoy, that published his defence of Wilson against the critics. So began an email correspondence with one of the partners in that publishing company, Michael Butterworth, that went on for several months. In mid-January, I decided to pitch the idea of doing a book of the interview to be published to coincide with the 50th anniversary of the publication of The Outsider, on 28 May 2006.

When it became clear that the timing and other aspects were difficult for 'traditional' book publication, Butterworth said he would love to do a print-on-demand book under a new imprint. I agreed, and then set about contacting Wilson, on Butterworth's suggestion, to see if he had any extra writing to add to it. Not only did Wilson immediately send several essays that he said we could use, but he also offered to look over the transcript. He said he would consider it "a major project", and go over the interview and make corrections and expand his ideas here and there.

The result is a book that truly reflects Wilson fifty years after *The Outsider*, and it is probably the most complete interview he has done. It began in the summer of 2005, and it was completed at the end of February 2006, fifty years minus two months after the publication of *The Outsider*.

Although Wilson combed through it, the interview contained in this book resembles the interview held in his home in Cornwall in July. The changes that Wilson made were mostly to clarify or expand an idea here or there, while keeping to the spirit of the original. For me as an interviewer and I hope for the reader as well, the interview shows what a tour de force Wilson is as a speaker.

Indeed, listening to Colin Wilson talk in an interview is virtually the same as reading a Colin Wilson book. This may be why some people find the person puzzling, and why others are as charmed by the person as they are by his writing.

I, in any case, was delighted not only with the interview, but the entire visit. It was a memorable one that I would like to share with the reader by describing some of the details of what I found of Colin Wilson's world, and which I had collected in notes the day after I visited his home:

He lives in the same house he has lived in since 1959, on a hill overlooking the sea. When I arrived, I commented on how nice and secluded it all was, as expected, but that I had nevertheless been surprised to see so many houses around.

"I know what you mean," he said.

I later noticed through his living room window that the hill to the sea was littered with the roofs of many houses, none of which had been there when he and his wife bought the place nearly fifty years before.

He lives with Joy and two dogs, Labrador types, which are very old – about thirteen for the one, and the other they do not know its age, as it was a stray. A parrot holds domain in a corner of the living room, where newspapers are spread out to catch its droppings – it has a box outside its cage where it likes to spend time. The door of the cage is open for free movement in and out. It seemed to spend most of its time hiding in the box, until about when I inquired about its existence and it emerged as if to see who I was.

The house is made of Cornish blocks, of cast concrete, plastered and pebble-dashed against winter storms. It looks built to last. Inside, it is filled in every room floor-to-ceiling with books and records, and hundreds of VCR tapes and many CDs. A quadraphonic sound system encircles the living room, which has a nice old fireplace in its centre. There are so many books that the Wilsons have had to build at least three large wooden cabins in the two-acre garden to contain the still-expanding collection.

There is also a two-room concrete building that used to be a stable or hen house, but which now has an apartment in it with kitchenette, bathroom, living room and bedroom. This is also full of books. Even the hallways in the main house have bookshelves at head-height. Both he and Joy are quite tall.

The house has four bedrooms, a basement and an attic, and they raised three children in it. The whole place is filled with spider webs, which, for a man who wrote a multi-volume novel called *Spider World*, makes sense. I dared not kill any spiders or destroy any webs, since he obviously likes them.

I did the interview while sitting in "Joy's chair", across from Wilson; the two of us either side of the fireplace. He related to me how at a previous interview Humphrey Carpenter had fallen asleep on the couch while Wilson was talking philosophy. It made me wonder if either I had a special place in having Joy's chair, or that he wanted to prevent the same thing from happening this time.

For a man who has been burned so often by the press, his openness and willingness to do a long interview shows that he has not allowed it to affect his natural friendliness.

Meeting an idol is a strange experience. I have probably read more of his books than of any other author, and Wilson would be the writer with whom I had the longest and longest lasting correspondence. While walking the dogs in a nearby forest he said he had probably corresponded with around ten thousand people since the publication of *The Outsider*.

I had a feeling before doing the interview and while reading the autobiography, that meeting him was something I would have to do now or never. He had aged by more than twenty years since I first contacted him, and I knew that time would fly on again and I might never meet him, even though he has often expressed the ambition of living to be ninety-five.

So when I did finally meet him, my first impressions were mixed. He had obviously been ill recently. He said it was a "mini stroke", and that he'd had two of them. He walked rather slowly, almost plodding along.

But when we went for a walk with the dogs in the forest, we took precarious pathways and wild fields, and hiked atop a large hill through brambles and bracken. He took a walking stick and insisted I have one as well. I felt like he was trying my mettle in the same way he describes in his autobiography that Robert Graves had tried his by climbing along a cliff face in Majorca then plunging into the sea.

He said in his autobiography that he has lived off an overdraft most of his life, often a massive one. But he owned an old Jaguar, while his wife had a newer car, and a Land Rover. He was lacking in nothing, it appeared. He used the Land Rover to go for walks in the woods along the cliffs, with the dogs in the back, and he used the Jaguar for shopping in Truro.

Once I had overcome the shock of seeing that a writer I had always thought of as young looked seventy-four, I was relieved to see that except for a problem with recent memory – like peoples' names, including my own on one occasion - he was one hundred percent there, fully in possession of all of his intellectual capacities.

In fact, I was massively impressed by his computer-like memory on things to do with literature and philosophy. The intellect that you meet is like the one you find in the books. He has references in his head to the most obscure writers and events, and I've never met anyone who could outdo me in one of the areas I'm most familiar with, which is the writers in Paris between the wars. While we were walking through the woods and still discussing books, I said Eugene Jolas had written a book called *A Narrow Street*, and he immediately corrected me and said it was Elliot Paul. Of course, I knew that, but I hadn't thought about Paul in years – neither would Wilson have done, but his memory was clearly better than mine.

He had a first edition of Joyce's *Ulysses*, or rather, a Shakespeare & Co edition, the 10th printing of the first edition, from around 1928.

He knew where most of the books in the house and its cabins were located, although he had forgotten at one point that he had moved *Ulysses* to a safer place in his own bedroom.

There were moments when I felt a kind of defensive fortress had been constructed around him and it took a while and some effort to break it down, although it did do so to an extent later in the interview. The early segments of the interview felt like a recital of his lectures of the past. I was happy to listen to it, though, because despite the needs of my article for shorter pithy personal quotes, it was interesting stuff, and like reading his books.

Moreover, I had read about his university lectures, and I wanted to see if he really was such a good speaker. In fact, he did sound like an excellent speaker, and I'd have liked to have attended one of his lectures – realising, of course, that that's what was happening now.

He never objected to me interrupting the flow with questions, observations and stories of my own. In fact, he even said when I left that he liked my stories and that I was welcome to return whenever I wanted. Yet there's an odd thing about his presence, in that it is not always apparent if he is in the least bit interested in you. But I think he simply has a way of masking his own observation of people and the world around him. Or perhaps it is that when someone is telling him a story he becomes so involved in listening to it that he becomes physically absent and therefore registers little in the way of body language to show that he is listening. Indeed, his writing itself certainly makes it apparent that he observes others, and in minute detail.

After the interview was finished and we had a drink, I played a Lenny Breau jazz CD for him, since it was an interesting recent discovery – that particular CD – and because his home was full of records of classical and jazz music. While I think he thought it was bizarre at first that I should suggest that we listen to this CD, he appeared to love the recording immediately and even told Joy what we were listening to, like a child full of enthusiasm for something new. Breau, of course, I told him, had been murdered.

Indeed, aside from his slow physical movement and the fact that he dressed in sweaters and a jacket and hat while indoors in the warm home – he commented that he was sensitive to the cold because he was taking blood-thinning tablets – once he spoke, he was the lively intellect we encounter in the books.

He was interrupted at the beginning of the interview by a telephone call from an editor at the Daily Mail who wanted him to write a story about the British military being given copies of the *Seven Pillars of Wisdom*. He had to turn down the offer as he was doing the interview with me, pointing out to the editorial assistant that I had travelled across Europe to see him. I switched off the recorder and told him maybe we could make the rest of the interview brief, and he could do his story, but he shook his head. "That wouldn't be fair to you." I said that at least we didn't have to talk for several hours, and he said, "No, no. It's all right. I enjoy talking." And he continued where he had been interrupted without missing a beat.

All the same, I felt he was battling against fatigue towards the end of the day, pushing himself to accommodate what I wanted from the interview, to do things properly and not give in to the fatigue.

Meeting his wife, I realised instantly who she was, having seen her photo in the autobiography. She does have a prominent nose, as he has described her. Her hair is short and white – his is not, although once he took his hat off later I saw he was losing hair – and she is thin and tall. In the end, I did not find her to be quite as 'vague' as he described her in his autobiography. She was 'simpler' than he is, in the sense of being less a roving intellectual spirit and more down to earth in the day-to-day sense, and obviously a good civilizing influence, or maybe stabilizing factor, in the household.

The three children have grown up and moved out, one living in London writing as a freelance and working with his father, another now working in the computer department of Oxford University, and the daughter is married to a Canadian wildlife expert on conservation, who now lives in the village, and has spent much time in Africa.

Wilson is obviously untouched by criticisms against him in some ways, but in others, he certainly has to steel himself to them to rise above the emotions when faced with them. In the interview he speaks of how he had overcome the rejection of his *Spider World* books by Bloomsbury without any problem. But as he talked about this, he described how, after feeling at first furious, he felt none of that sinking of the heart that usually accompanies negative thoughts.

"It was then I suddenly realised that I had, over the past year, achieved a little of what Gurdjieff calls 'essence', a feeling of inner solidness. Gurdjieff said that the only way to create this is through what he called 'intentional suffering', like the painful self-disciplines of the ascetic. This is the only reliable way of overcoming the laziness and weakness that does its best to hide inside you."

He is a curious mixture of pride, self-belief and confidence, but fear and self-doubt do become evident. He leapt in fear when I surprised him in his garage preparing the car – as anyone will do when taken by surprise from time to time – but he felt the need to explain that he is so deeply absorbed in his thoughts that the unexpected brings him a scare.

In fact, he said, he always "leaps a mile in the air" if someone appears unexpectedly when he thinks he is alone. He said this is because the panic attacks that he describes in his autobiography had to be overcome by teaching himself not to 'leak' energy.

As his defender, Meadley, intelligently pointed out: if Wilson is an optimist, then he is one who is constantly fighting against pessimism. He is only too aware of the pessimism that pervades modern society, which is why he fights it – the opposite of Pollyannaism. Seeing Wilson in person, I agree with Meadley – but even reading the autobiography makes it obvious that this is not something that was easily come by.

I noted that although he has gotten rid of his Leicester accent, it occasionally slips back in for particular words. Most actors do this as a matter of course, but it is less usual in writers – he explained that it came out of his intense dislike of everything to do with his Leicester background. But there is something of the professor about it too. It has an otherworldliness to it that the Colin Wilson writing style does not have. In other words, his speaking voice sounds less down-to-earth than his writing – although that aspect does not come across in the meaning or choice of words, which, as I say, sounds like the way he writes.

The recorded interview went on for over three hours. It almost began as soon as we sat down and before I had turned on the recorder, so I interrupted his talk, pressed the record button, and recapped a little in my question.

The Interview: One

BRAD SPURGEON: I'm interested in what you said just then about people having to work hard to reach higher levels of being, of achievement, etcetera.
COLIN WILSON: It involves putting a kind of effort into it that is extremely difficult for human beings. And the reason – which is something that has always preoccupied me – is the fact that we are ninety-nine percent robot, ninety-nine percent mechanical. Gurdjieff's teaching starts off from this recognition – that we are almost entirely mechanical. But that is also an advantage as far as human beings are concerned. The robot makes us the most efficient animal on earth. We have succeeded in packing so much learning into our computer memories that we can almost live completely automatically. But, of course, in order to

1

do anything really worthwhile, you need to get beyond that automatic response. Get out of the robot. And that is what has always interested me so much.

BS: What it's really about is that...

> [*Here the telephone rings and he curses, but it turns out to be the Daily Mail newspaper wanting him to write the piece about the British Army giving out TE Lawrence's* Seven Pillars of Wisdom *to troops*]

> [*I tell him that it was one of my favourite films as a child but that I had tried and given up – as a child – reading the* Seven Pillars of Wisdom]

CW: You ought to read my piece about him in *The Outsider*. That's why I find him so interesting, because he's the typical outsider figure.

BS: I did read that. There were several other people in the book I didn't know anything about, though – other than their names – like Nijinsky.

CW: When I wrote *The Outsider*, Hermann Hesse wasn't known. I was the first person to write about Hermann Hesse in English. Of course, in no time at all, after the success of *The Outsider*, Hermann Hesse was being quoted all over the place and people in America were writing books and theses about him... But they never quoted me, because *The Outsider* had been a little too popular.

BS: When I was in high school in the early 1970s, everyone was reading Hesse.

CW: I discovered Hermann Hesse simply because he got the Nobel Prize for a book called *The Glass Bead Game* which I found in my local library when I was in my early twenties, and proceeded to get hold of everything I could find – *Steppenwolf, Demian*. In the British Museum reading room I took the opportunity to read everything else that had been translated, like this little essay *Glimpse into Chaos* which Eliot had quoted in the notes to *The Waste Land*. Part of the reason for the success of *The Outsider* was that it was so full of writers most people knew nothing about. The result was that even the intellectual critics found it interesting and informative.

BS: When did you develop your theories of optimism? I don't think you could be considered a natural optimist, could you?

CW: I don't know. In my teens, I certainly came close to suicide. But don't forget what I've just been saying: that anybody who has to pull his cart out of the mud becomes an optimist as a matter of survival. To begin with, you see, I became an optimist because I was fascinated by science from the age of ten, and it seemed to me that science was going to transform human existence. An uncle gave me *The Marvels and Mysteries of Science* when I was ten years old, and it was like a revelation. Then I discovered chemistry when I was given a chemistry set for my eleventh birthday. Naturally, I soon came across the science fiction novels of HG Wells, who became the first great influence on my mind. Wells also believed that the human race will eventually solve all its problems through science. So by the time I was twelve or thirteen, I just was totally optimistic because I felt that science would one day turn us into 'men like gods'. Then I went through the usual period of teenage misery and confusion, which turned me into a nihilist and made me feel that it's all an illusion. But then I slowly outgrew that. As Nietzsche said, "I made my philosophy out of my will to health." And that's how I gradually became an optimist. I should add that the fiction of GK Chesterton, particularly *The Man Who Was Thursday*, where he speaks of 'absurd good news', was a major influence.

BS: It's interesting that writers like Wells and Shaw were optimists and were also considered great intellects at the time. But then pessimistic literature took over, didn't it? And these people were…

CW: Well, no, what happened is rather more complicated. Up until about 1740 literature had not really taken off. The novel had only just got started. It's true there were novelists like Mrs Aphra Behn, but what they called novels were preposterous fantasies, with names like *Orinoco*, set in weird islands in the Pacific. And Defoe's novels were really reportage. But then this London printer Samuel Richardson did a book about how to write letters. This was quite a success and he thought, well, one could actually write a proper novel based on this technique. So he proceeded to write a novel called *Pamela*. Which was about a maidservant, who goes to work in a big house, and writes to her mother: "The master's terribly nice to me." Then she wakes up to what he really wants. "Oh dear, the master just came in and put his hand on my breast and said, 'Pamela, I have a feeling we're going to be great friends.'" And of course he spends the rest of the novel

4

trying to fling her on beds and screw her. The novel was an overnight success, the first bestseller. The truth is that it was really a kind of highly moralistic pornography, and readers sat there gasping [*he makes sounds of heavy breathing*]. And of course at the end he hasn't succeeded in screwing her, and he marries her because he's so impressed by goodness and virtue. The end was really pure romance, like Daphne Du Maurier's *Rebecca*. And so Pamela became a success all over Europe. And this was in 1740. And then of course Richardson went on to repeat the formula with a novel called *Clarissa*, also written in letters, where the heroine does get raped. I think the novel was the most important human invention since the wheel.

That was because it was a kind of magic carpet. People could sit down in their armchairs, and fly away into other people's lives. You weren't trapped in your own skin any more – you could spend hours being somebody else, even someone of the opposite sex. Soon writing novels had turned into an industry – Fielding and Smollett and Sterne – and all over Europe people were taking off on the magic carpet and floating out of their boring lives and into someone else's.

Now the nearest equivalent of the novel in earlier centuries had been the playhouse. But that cost more effort. Now a bored country housewife could hide in the window seat and become Pamela for the day. She didn't have to spend her time telling off the cook, and visiting the poor with baskets of food. She could spend a month at sea with Peregrine Pickle.

Now this was all very well – wonderful in fact – but the problem was that when they came back to earth again they came down with a horrible bump, and looked out of the window and said: "Oh dear, it's not nearly as nice as fiction." I remember my little daughter Sally saying after we'd taken her to see *The Wizard of Oz*, "I wish there *was* a land over the rainbow", and looking terribly sad. And that was a problem that became more and more obvious after the invention of the novel. All those romantic writers were fed up with the real world. That's why so many romantic poets became alcoholics or took drugs, or committed suicide. They had become more sensitive, more intelligent, more 'spiritual'. But they couldn't stand the real world because they'd discovered that the world of imagination was far more interesting. In *The Shadowy Waters*, Yeats said, "What the world's million lips are searching for *must* be substantial somewhere." And yet it seemed horribly obvious that it wasn't 'substantial' – it was just a dream.

What had happened was that a tremendous gap had suddenly opened up between real life and the life of the imagination. But since Goethe's *Young Werther* had triggered the new Romantic Movement in the 1770s, a whole generation of poets and novelists had taught themselves to live in the world of the imagination – in England Coleridge and Byron and Shelley, in Germany Hoffmann, Jean Paul, Ludwig Tieck, all of them writing around 1800, and who deserve to be remembered because they're so good. I discovered Jean Paul in my early twenties and could see why his contemporaries thought he was as important as Shakespeare, and why Mahler called his first symphony after his novel *Titan* – an incredible work. You know, when you read the early romantics you can really take off on a magic carpet and go into other worlds. Hoffmann is particularly good.

BS: ETA Hoffmann.

CW: Yes. And so suddenly there was this great dichotomy opening up like a chasm. They felt forced to choose. Did they want boredom and everyday life – life with a small 'l' – or did they want a world that seemed to vibrate with hidden depths of meaning?

There was only one problem. Rejecting everyday life and its boring triviality meant they were, in a sense, choosing death. That's what it amounted to. Which is why those 19th Century Outsiders died off like flies – of tuberculosis or in terrible accidents. And that went on happening to the end of the century. That was what was in the back of my mind in my first book *The Outsider* – Keats, Byron, Shelley, Beddoes, Rimbaud and the rest, all utterly miserable. And in the 1890s there were the poets and artists Yeats called 'the tragic generation' – Ernest Dowson, Lionel Johnson, Aubrey Beardsley, James Thompson. Yeats himself probably expected to die young as a punishment for rejecting the everyday world in favour of fairylands and ancient Irish legends… you know, "Come away human child to the waters in the wild with a fairy, hand in hand for the world's more full of weeping than you can understand." The result was that by the end of the 19th Century, an enormous pall of gloom had descended over the whole intellectual landscape.

The pessimism of the romantics could be labelled Romanticism Mark 1. But then along came a group who called themselves existentialists, and who dated back to the 1850s, Kierkegaard and Nietzsche. Their approach was less emotional than intellectual. But existentialism is almost as pessimistic as romanticism – in fact, you could label it Romanticism Mark II. Their vision of the world is summarised in Sartre's comment, "It is meaningless that we live and meaningless that we die – man is a useless passion." And so it goes on. It is true that existentialism succeeds in being slightly less gloomy than romanticism – Camus says in *The Myth of Sisyphus* that Sisyphus has to spend eternity rolling a rock uphill and watching it roll down again – yet nevertheless, we must imagine Sisyphus happy, for he still possesses inner freedom, the freedom of his own mind. Existentialism is grim. But its basic atmosphere is still one of pessimism. The black clouds are still hovering over the landscape.

Now Nietzsche had said, "I made my philosophy out of my will to health." And it was perfectly apparent to me – when I was in my early teens and also suffering from total nihilism – it was perfectly obvious to me that there had to be some major change of direction. We had to put pessimism behind us. And it struck me that the real problem of the romantics was not so much genuine pessimism as a sort of shallow self-pity. "How dare life treat me like this?" But the existentialists turned it into something much more intellectual and solid, and therefore easier to attack. Once you can see something clearly, you can begin to think about how to change it. And that, I felt, has to be my own starting point.

When I began writing in my mid-teens, existentialism was the new intellectual fashion. But of course, I disliked its pessimism. Hemingway's *Old Man and the*

Sea came out about then, and it's phrase "A man can be destroyed but not defeated", struck me as the essence of existentialism. But it made me realise that I had no intention of being defeated or destroyed. And it was then that I saw clearly that I had to create a new kind of existentialism – you might call it Romanticism Mark III – that went one step further. The romantics had ended in defeat, the existentialists had ended in stoical despair, and I felt that it should be possible to create a philosophy that was fundamentally optimistic.

What I didn't realise at that time was that it had already been done for me – by Edmund Husserl, the man who laid the foundations of existentialism. Because his recognition that perception is intentional – that you fire your attention like an arrow at a target – meant that we have a kind of invisible archer inside us. There is, so to speak, another 'you' behind the 'you' of everyday consciousness. Kant had called this hidden 'you' the Transcendental Ego – which really meant the soul. But Sartre's first little book, *The Transcendence of the Ego*, declares that perception is, indeed, intentional. But there's no hidden ego behind it. Just emptiness. We react to the world like penny-in-the-slot machines. Yet in spite of that, Sartre said, we are free. "We are as free as you like, but helpless."

No that it absurd. Freedom is nothing if it is not freedom to act. And during the war, when he was in the Resistance, Sartre changed his mind and decided that we are, after all, free to make choices. But you won't find that in his major work *Being and Nothingness*. That concentrates entirely on our self-deceptions, which he called 'mauvaise foi', bad faith.

I could see that he had simply made a philosophical error. Worse than that, a kind of schoolboy howler. By getting rid of the Transcendental Ego, he had left philosophy in the same old mess. But what he was saying was illogical – that yes, perception *is* intentional, yes, it is fired at a target like an arrow. But there's no archer. The outside world pulls our intentions towards it, as the moon pulls the tides. That is absurd. How can a non-existential archer fire an arrow? And as soon as you get rid of that piece of muddled thinking, you have a basically optimistic existentialism.

We are back to the problem that screwed up the romantics. Byron said in *The Prisoner of Chillon*: "Eternal spirit of the chainless mind, brightest in dungeons, liberty thou art." He was saying that freedom is something that's inside us – you can't take it away. And Camus was saying the same about Sisyphus – we must imagine him happy. Nevertheless, if you feel that there's no way of grasping your freedom physically, escaping from Chillon, then you're going to remain basically pretty gloomy.

And that has been the problem of every philosopher in history. In the last analysis, they've all been pessimistic. Always. Aristotle said that it is better not to have been born, and death is better than life. Socrates says that in dying he's merely fulfilling the philosopher's destiny because the philosopher spends his life trying to separate the body and the soul. And so in dying he's merely doing this. And so it goes on.

BS: Well Aristotle was looking for the Golden Mean, as well, wasn't he? A kind of equilibrium.

CW: Oh yes, but basically Aristotle did feel – as the

Greeks tended to – that life was pretty hard, as indeed it was for the ancient Greeks. If you and I could go back to ancient Athens now we'd find life pretty bloody. I mean, for example the average working man had practically nothing to eat except olives.

Anyway, just to recap: when Hemingway said a man can be destroyed but not defeated, I thought, that's all very well, but I don't want to be defeated or destroyed. I thought there must be some other way. So when I really settled down to studying this, I could see that there was a basic fallacy in Sartre and Camus and Heidegger and Jasper. The fallacy lay in their failure to understand the actual foundation of the problem.

Now as I say, existentialism was based upon the work of Husserl, who had come up with the realisation of intentionality – that whenever you look at something it doesn't merely walk in through your eyes and imprint itself on your brain. You have to shoot your perception like an arrow. But if you don't pull back the bowstring far enough, if you're feeling tired or lazy, then the arrow merely falls at your feet, and everything looks dull and boring. That's what made the romantics despair. You don't see it. For example, it's like reading a paragraph in a paper without attention and having to go back and re-read it. You have to direct intentionality towards whatever you're seeing if you want to see it.

Now what follows from that is quite clear: that the *more* you direct intentionality at things the more you see. So if you walk through the world in a sort of semi-mechanical sloppy state of mind, you don't see the same world that is seen, let us say, by a mystic like William

Blake or Van Gogh – who were absolutely wide-awake. That's what Aldous Huxley saw when he took mescaline – the world as it is, without the misery and gloom that we unconsciously impose on it. It was like taking off a pair of dark glasses, and realising that it's really quite a sunny day. That this external reality, which we take for granted as being merely there, is in fact incredibly exciting. That it's pulsating and glowing and vibrating, and quite unlike anything we can imagine.

Well this seemed to me to be the basic answer to this whole problem of pessimistic existentialism. That they'd made a quite simple mistake in philosophical thinking. Their mistake was in failing to see that this gloom which they took for granted as being justifiable, was in fact, merely intentional. They were *imposing* it upon things. It was their own minds that were painting things black.

Intentionality is basically what Tom Sawyer does when he's painting the fence. He whistles vigorously as he paints, people come along, watch him, and say, "Hey, can we do a bit?" And finally he's been given a whole pile of things, like a penknife and a ball of string and a dead cat, just to allow them to whitewash the fence. He's done all this by persuading them that it's *worth doing.* And Mark Twain says, "Work is that which one is compelled to do; play is that which one is not compelled to do." They're intentional.

All this means that you could transform your life, make it fascinating and delightful, merely by changing your mental attitude towards it. That's a tremendously important discovery. A discovery that Sartre and Camus never made because they took it for granted that the external world is really pretty bloody and awful.

BS: Well, theirs is a popular view as well, isn't it?

CW: Yeah, and Hemingway too with his sort of natural gloom.

So what I wanted to do was to try to create a philosophy upon a completely new foundation. Whereas in the past optimism had been regarded as sort of rather shallow – because, "Oh well, it's just your temperament, you happen to be just a cheerful sort of person" – what I wanted to do was to establish that, in fact, it is the pessimists who are allowing all kinds of logical errors to creep into their work. And that as soon as you refuse to allow these errors to creep in, what you end up with is an entirely optimistic point of view. So what I've tried to do is for the first time in history, in a way, to create a truly optimistic philosophy. I mean it's just never been done. At least, it's been done by one single man: Nietzsche, who may well be the greatest philosopher in history.

BS: I haven't read him.

CW: Well, it doesn't matter if you haven't read him. Read my bit in *The Outsider* about him. That will tell you what you need to know.

BS: I read Kierkegaard.

CW: Well the interesting thing about Kierkegaard is simply that he was basically a sort of romantic, and romantics naturally dislike the world because it is not nearly as interesting as their imagination. And also he disliked Danish society intensely because he was genuinely religious. Rather as Kafka was. Mind you, religion is very often the result of gloom, the result of pessimism. And Kierkegaard as a consequence, got very impatient with Hegel's philosophy, and Hegel in fact is one of the greatest of all philosophers because he also succeeded in creating a kind of optimism.

But Kierkegaard said, "Damn Hegel. He's created this giant philosophical system, which is in the last analysis optimistic, but so what? His system doesn't suit me at all. I don't fit into it. Force me to swallow Hegel's system and you negate me completely. It's like a huge, loose-fitting suit that doesn't keep me warm. "

He said that Hegel's philosophy is rather like a cup of tea that's been made out of tea from which tea has already been made half a dozen times. He also said that as a guide to living, it's rather like trying to find your way around Copenhagen with a map of the world on which Copenhagen is the size of a pinpoint.

What he wanted was a big map of Copenhagen, where you can really say, "Ah, that's where I am." Like those Tube maps which say, "You are here." And his feeling was that once you've done that – and said, "OK, this is where I am, I am here" – you can make a start on getting where you want to go.

But where *did* Kierkegaard want to go? He was deeply religious, which means he was also a kind of mystic. He longed for a kind of bird's eye view of existence that would tell him what human beings are doing here. He wrote a novel in which he said: "Why wasn't I consulted before being thrown down into this confusing world? Who is responsible? I want to see the director. Take me to see the director."

So it was no good Hegel telling him that the purpose of history is for man to evolve into a god. He wanted to know what to do *now*, right at this moment. He wanted a 'system' all right, but an existential system, not an aerial view of Copenhagen from outer space.

But Hegel was right all the same. Philosophy means taking an aerial view. If you stay on the ground, you'll never get any further – particularly if, like Kierkegaard, you've got weak legs and aren't very good at walking.

To put it another way, he was rather like a painter who's extremely short-sighted and has to paint with his nose within two inches of the canvas. The only problem is that he can never see his canvas properly, because every time he steps back to see how he's getting on, he's so short-sighted that he can't see the whole thing and has to keep peering at it from two inches again. So what's the answer? He needs an optician to say: "I've got some things here called spectacles. You put those on and stand back and you'll be able to see it as a whole." That's what Kierkegaard needed: philosophical spectacles.

But he never found any, so he didn't really do much good. You see, if you can't get out of Hegel's position, looking at the map and never deciding where you are, you finish like those two tramps in *Waiting for Godot*, feeling "There's nothing to be done."

Beckett is a terrible example of a man who found himself in Kierkegaard's position, asking to see the director but feeling sure there isn't a director, and life's all a rotten joke, and spending the rest of his days telling the rest of us that it's meaningless and we'd do better to lie down and die. Beckett is the apogee of two centuries of romantic pessimism, the furthest you can go. To me, the amazing thing is that they gave this bastard the Nobel Prize for telling us to lie down and die.

You might say: "So what? He didn't do any harm." But his type poison our culture, our civilization. Tell Beckett that the poles are melting and we're all going to be flooded, and he says "Good. That's just what we deserve."

Anyway, my feeling was that once you recognise the damage done by this kind of sloppy thinking, and begin to see the fallacies in Hemingway and Sartre and Beckett, you begin to consider the alternative. And with a little luck, you end by recognising that it *is* possible to base your outlook on optimism and the conviction that life can only be understood in terms of evolution.

One of the earliest and greatest influences on me was Gurdjieff, and Gurdjieff's conviction that we are basically entirely mechanical – or almost entirely mechanical – and fast asleep into the bargain. The first thing we need to do is to wake up and cease to be mechanical.

> [*Joy comes to say she is leaving and has left a note for someone – the gardener, I believe, since later in the interview I hear a lawnmower cutting the grass outside. She says she will return as soon as possible*]
>
> [*Wilson is now well into his stride, and goes on without pausing for breath:*]

CW: So you see, all of this fascinates me very much, because for me the really great question is how one *can* wake up. We get these really wonderful moments, which Maslow called 'peak experiences', in which the

16

whole world is self-evidently good.

BS: Wordsworth had a word for them as well…

CW: The glory and the freshness of a dream…

BS: Spots of time …

CW: And Proust called them 'moments bienheureux'. These sudden moments of absolute sheer happiness, which are in a sense totally illogical. The moments when, as Proust said: "I had ceased to feel mediocre, accidental, mortal." He knew perfectly well that you can spend most of your time feeling that the world is absolutely awful, and then, out of the blue, one of these moments of intense happiness descends upon you because you have smelled something like the whitewash in a lavatory in the Champs Elysées, and quite suddenly you're full of an irrational wild happiness… [*He raises his voice loudly in joy at the end of that sentence*] …What Chesterton called, "Absurd good news." Well the interesting question for me is that if this is true, then therefore our usual extremely gloomy view of things is not true…

BS: 'True' meaning 'real'?

CW: True, yes, like one and one is two. Real, yes. Which raises the really interesting question. If that is so, how could we live in such a way that you could intensify this feeling? As we have seen, the problem with the unfortunate romantics is that they would get these wonderful feelings when suddenly everything seemed wonderful, and then they'd wake up the next morning and look around and wonder what they were talking about. They'd give a groan and bury their faces in their hands, and say, "What the hell did I mean? What's wonderful about this bloody lousy world?" Now that is the real problem. How do you hang on to the moments of insight, to the peak experiences?

When Abe Maslow talked to me about peak experiences in the 1960s, I realised suddenly that he'd gone a mile beyond Sartre and Hemingway and Beckett, and discovered something of terrific importance. Abe said that as a psychologist he'd got sick of studying sick people because they talked about nothing but their sickness. Therefore, he decided to try studying healthy people and see what they were like. And he told me he'd immediately discovered something that nobody had ever discovered before because nobody had thought of studying healthy people: that healthy people had with great frequency feelings for which he invented the term peak experiences. Just experiences of sudden bubbling overwhelming happiness, in which you say, "My God, isn't it wonderful?"

You have to understand that peak experiences were not necessarily great mystical experiences. A hostess looking around at the room after she'd given a very successful party, and looking at the cigarette ashes on the carpet, and the red wine on the sofa, nevertheless thought, "My God, that was a good party!" and went into the peak experience. A mother giving breakfast to her husband and children when a beam of sunlight suddenly came in through the window and she thought, "My God, aren't I lucky," and went into the peak experience. A marine who had spent ten years in the Pacific without ever seeing a girl, came back to civilization, at base camp, and saw a nurse and went into a peak experience because he said he suddenly realised that *women are different from men.*

The peak experience suddenly makes you see things which are true but which one doesn't notice normally because one's so mechanical.

I asked Abe how could you recreate the peak experience at will and Abe said, "Unfortunately, it can't be done. They come when they want to, and they go when they want to." And I said, "But don't you see you're contradicting yourself? You're saying that human beings have some kind of power over reality, some power to grasp that everything is good, and you're taking an optimistic view as opposed to Freud's total pessimism about life and civilization. And yet now you're telling me there's no way of inducing peak experiences." And Abe said, "Well I'm afraid I haven't come across one."

Well that, I suppose, made me aware of my central goal: How can one induce peak experiences simply by wanting to? And little by little I learned the trick. It's a kind of peculiar form of concentration. What it means basically is that you're able to focus until you suddenly experience that sense that everything is good.

Hesse said, in *Journey to the East,* that the narrator discovered that "it is attention to small things that refreshes us and increases our strength." In other words, makes us capable of having peak experiences. But why? What exactly does it do?

Well, psychological illness could be described as allowing your vital batteries to go flat. When we're bored and tired, we simply 'let go', and go into a mechanical state. The moment we start doing something *with interest*, it's exactly like putting your car battery on charge, or just driving the car so the battery re-charges itself. So that's what Hesse's narrator had learned.

Above all, of course, it's a matter of recognising that the real trouble with human beings is that we leak. We go around leaking energy in the same way that someone who has slashed their wrists would go around leaking blood. The moment something interests you, you focus on it, and the leak closes automatically.

And this applies particularly to teenagers – they go around in a permanent state of misery due to leakage. Their heart's always sinking, they're all saying, "Oh my God. How awful." And blushing with embarrassment and getting into terrible states about things.

Well, once you can actually get over that and recognise that this is not necessary, suddenly you begin to see the possibility of achieving a different state of mind, a kind of steady focus, which means that you see things as good, as positive. And that therefore you can recreate the peak experience by simply wanting to.

I don't know whether you read the chapter in the autobiography…

BS: I read the whole thing.

CW: Well, in the chapter on Maslow I talk about a man called Syd Banks. Syd Banks was an ordinary bloke, just a working man, who one day had a sudden revelation. What happened was that he said to a friend of his, "Oh God, I'm so unhappy." And the friend said, "You're not unhappy, Syd – you just think you are." And he said, "What did you say?" And it suddenly hit him like a bomb, that this is true, that all our unhappiness is due to our own thoughts. Or rather due to the way that without even noticing it, we shade the world, we allow our prejudices to sneak in, and turn everything dark, like putting on a pair of sunglasses. Now that's what phenomenology is about.

Husserl said: "The problem with philosophy is we are continually allowing our prejudices to sneak into our perceptions without recognising them as prejudices." What we've got to do is to find a way of looking at the world so coolly and detachedly that we see it almost as a series of symbols and don't react to it at all with feelings. He called this method phenomenology. And phenomenology is really a kind of detached observation. And there's a particular technique for doing this kind of detached observation. What it means, eventually, is that you don't plunge into emotional judgements in the way that, say, Sartre or Heidegger do, and say, "Anybody can see that human life is continuous frustration, or the world's meaningless, man is a useless passion."

Even if you read Heidegger's *Being and Time*, which is his major philosophical work, you can go through it picking up things which he claims are self-evidently true, and which are not self-evidently true. They are just his own emotions and personal reactions. It makes me think of a girl suffering from menstrual pains, and telling you, "Surely it's obvious to anyone that life is grim and miserable". And you want to say, "No, no, it's just your menstrual pains."

BS: I found much of what you write very close to things I discovered myself but wouldn't have put in the same words, would not be able to articulate in the same way. I was interested in the mescaline thing you wrote about in your autobiography, with both your own experience in having tried mescaline and Aldous Huxley's.

As a teenager, I had – like many others of my

21

generation in the early 1970s – tried mescaline and other hallucinogenic drugs. But I should give you a little of the psychological background for what I want to say... my mother was an adopted child in the 1930s, who had been rejected also by this second family at the age of seven and returned to the orphanage. She was then taken back again later by that same family, but you can imagine the scars of being put up for adoption twice. Basically, she was depressed for much of her life and had a fairly black view of life. So I grew up myself feeling somehow that it was normal to be depressed all the time and to be negative – particularly as a teenager.

So now back to the drugs: With the drugs, I had experiences that were both the extraordinarily wonderful experience where the world is the most extraordinary place, much as you describe. Pleasant hallucinations. But I also had the absolute nightmare experience such as, for instance, I used to smoke a pipe as a teenager, and I once during a rock concert at which I had taken drugs, hallucinated that I was eating the pipe, and then I was eating my tongue, and then my hand had fallen off my wrist into a bloody mess in my lap. It was an absolute horror, but you believe entirely in the reality of what you see and feel.

Well ultimately, one night – this was all happening when I was seventeen – I sat down in my bedroom, and I had taken some pure THC crystals – the chemical basis of marijuana and hashish – and I sat up all night and said to myself, there's something wrong with my life. And I analysed this. I did not do it in words, but with a pencil and paper on which I drew lines connecting the high and low points of the drugs with the emotional events in my life at the time. And I saw that in my life I was either very high, bubbly and manic, or very low and depressed. And I then realised that with the drug, the good and the bad experiences coincided with the periods when I was either going into it in a happy, manic state – and that was when it was the extraordinary world – or going into it in the depressive state and that's when it was hell…

CW: That's what Aldous Huxley recognised. He said in *The Doors of Perception*, that if you went into it taking a bad and negative attitude, you would end up totally convinced you were in hell.

BS: I didn't realise he had written that. Although I think I read the book at the time. But then I realised also during that night when I analysed what was going on, that it all indicated that there was something wrong with me. That there was either hell or there was heaven. And furthermore, that the reason I was taking the drugs was to reach this Nirvana, but that I shouldn't be using a substance to reach it, I should be there naturally. So I suddenly at that moment recognised for the first time clearly that negative emotion was in fact destructive. And positive emotion, or optimism, was constructive. But also that I must try to achieve these states without artificial stimulation – in the sense of a drug, because you do not do anything but throw it into your mouth, and thereby avoid dealing with the underlying problem that is blocking the route to natural happiness – and that there must be a way to achieving what you're talking about naturally.

And so I ended up seeking this state of what you

might call 'a glow of optimism' by exerting effort. By trying to construct something, rather than destruct. At the time, it was nothing more than learning how to juggle, and practicing the circus arts – although I later channelled it into reading and writing. But basically, it was a recognition that I was unbalanced and had a negative view of the world which was destructive. But also, once I had this understanding that depression is negative and bad, destructive, and that I must try to achieve an equilibrium, ultimately I said that just understanding that fact is a positive development – and you have said that in a way in your books as well. But I also decided that I should test my theory of having made emotional progress by continuing to try drugs a few times just to be sure. I did not want this apparent understanding of an emotional truth to in fact be nothing but an excuse to flee from a bad drug experience.

And indeed, once I'd realised the root of my problems and where I was going, I was able to take the drugs and be normal – neither have a horrendous experience nor a great one. So once I was satisfied that I truly understood what was happening, and understood why I had taken them in the first place – as a way of seeking emotional fulfilment – I then stopped taking drugs and have never touched them again and have never had any desire to do so. I have tried to reach the higher states of consciousness – or simple emotional stability and the state of productive optimism – through the natural methods of work, outlook, discipline and relationships. And this is one of the things that interests me in your philosophy, that you can naturally try to achieve this sort of thing.

CW: Well it's a fairly simple business in a sense, and the key to it is in my book *Beyond the Occult* – which I regard as my most important book – where I talk about the seven levels of consciousness.*

The point being that our ordinary normal human level, the level we take for granted as the norm, is the fourth level of consciousness. Below that, consciousness gets duller and duller. Level Three is what Sartre called 'nausea'. You and I at the moment are about halfway up Level Four. The lower half of Level Four is nevertheless still bloody hard work, there's that feeling which was expressed by Christina Rossetti, "Does the road wind uphill all the way? Right to the very end?" And then, round about half way up Level Four, where we are at present, you begin to get that feeling that we're free, that effort makes a difference, that feeling, "You *can* win", and a surge of optimism. Quite suddenly you've got a sense of motivation and drive, and then the obstacles seem to evaporate, and you begin to get this increasing certainty that everything's going to be OK.

Now it's quite difficult to pull yourself out of the pessimistic level into the optimistic level, that is, beyond Level Four-and-a-half. But once you're there, it's not terribly difficult to stay there, and even go higher.

Level Five is in fact the peak experience. The peak experience is a kind of stopgap between Level Four and Level Five. That sudden feeling of 'absurd good news'. And once you get to that stage you find it quite easy to maintain, because optimism tends to be self-perpetuating. Level Five is what I tend to call 'holiday consciousness', or 'spring morning consciousness', because we get it on a spring morning when you're setting out on holiday and driving down a country road with the feeling, "My God, isn't everything lovely."

Now there's no reason why human beings, once they've understood how to do it, should not be able to maintain that state of mind all the time.

BS: What interests me is how you say that effort is necessary to reach these states.

CW: Well yes, it does require what Gurdjieff calls 'intentional suffering.' Not meaning pain and misery, but real effort until it hurts.

I made that discovery when I was around sixteen or seventeen when I discovered the *Bhagavad Gita*. At the time I was stuck in a job that bored me, working in a lab, and every morning I woke up with a sinking feeling at the thought of going back to it. Then I came across the *Gita* in a local bookshop, and I'd seen it referred to in Eliot's essays. So I followed its instructions. I'd sit cross-legged on my bedroom floor at half past six in the morning, and just concentrate, focusing my mind for about half an hour. And it charged me up with energy, so that for the rest of the day I felt bubbly. I'd simply recharged my batteries.

What I've discovered as I've got older is that you can get into this state of focused energy and stay in it all day. And even over the past year I've discovered new methods of doing it. Of course, I'm not claiming that its some mystical state of higher consciousness. But if ordinary consciousness is four point five, then this is about four point seven.

When I was pretty sure that the autobiography was going to be a great success – because it's a fucking masterpiece [*He laughs a bit as I agree wholeheartedly*] – it's as good a book as I've ever written – and when it, on the contrary, got viciously attacked, I thought, well I know *I'm* not wrong. Obviously the times are out of joint. I'm not so stupid as not to know when I've written a good book. Yet things continued to be difficult.

After that, I'd decided I wanted to do this book about the Angry Young Men, just for the sake of the record, and I began contacting several of the living survivors of the movement – Alan Sillitoe, Christopher Logue, Doris Lessing. I wrote three chapters of this book, and my agent submitted them to a publisher who had asked to see them, and I was pretty sure that it was good stuff and shouldn't have too much trouble finding a publisher. Instead, again to my absolute astonishment, several publishers turned it down.

BS: Could that have been connected to the few bad reviews of the autobiography?

CW: No, no, nothing to do with that. [*Chuckling as he says*:] Connected to Saturn being in my House, that's what it was. But after I'd had the latest rejection I naturally felt a bit gloomy. Then, about half an hour later, I was sitting in this chair – it was early evening – and I'd totally forgotten about it, watching the news on television. Then my mind came back to the rejection, and I was very interested to note that I didn't experience any of that feeling of sinking of the heart that you get when you remember something discouraging. And I thought, "This is interesting. No sinking of the heart at all."

The answer, of course, lay in the concentration

exercises. I do them whenever I'm out walking, or driving to the supermarket. In other words, I've changed mentally over the past year so that I am a few degrees higher than before the autobiography came out. I've slowly taught myself to remain in a permanent state of optimism – or realism, if you like – this curious ability to focus upon external reality. Now it's true that I've been doing this for years. Now I can see that it can be done quite deliberately by a kind of effort, almost like doing a push-up.

BS: What sort of effort are you using?

CW: Basically it amounts to attention. You know the story about the Zen Master Ikkyu, when a workman asked him to write something significant on his tablet, he wrote 'Attention'. And the workman said, "That's not very significant, can't you write something more?" So he wrote, 'Attention, attention'. The workman said, "What does attention mean?" And Ikkyu said, "Attention means attention."

Here's an example. One day I was out on the sun-trap, where we keep the duplicator, and I had to duplicate a whole book I had just finished about Aleister Crowley. I was doing this in the usual mechanical state of mind, you know, come on, "Let's get this over with." Then I suddenly thought, "This is going to take me at least an hour, and that's an hour gone straight out of my life if I just stand here mechanically thinking, 'Oh come on, let's get this over with.'" So I quite deliberately caught myself, and concentrated and focused totally, and within a quarter of an hour I was doing it in a state of heightened energy.

That sudden realisation that you can do this,

that you can induce the peak experience by focused attention, was a new discovery. And I've continued to explore this. Yesterday, for example, I did a pretty hard day's work – particularly for someone of my age, you know, a couple of hours work of writing, steady creative writing, is quite enough when you're seventy-four. But I'd spent the whole morning having to read through a rather thick book about a murderer called DeBardeleben, who was so clever at covering his crimes that even reading about them is like hacking your way through a jungle. By the time I finished, my eyes were aching and my head spinning. Then I had to go ahead and write about it all afternoon.

Now it so happened that that morning I went to use the phone and I found the phone wasn't working. I thought, "Oh dear, I hope I can get this into order before Brad arrives, otherwise he's going to ring up and get no reply." And I rang up the telephone exchange and they said, "How many extensions have you got?" So I said, "We've got the main phone and two extensions." They said, "Well, isolate all three and test them one by one." So here I was trying to get on with my writing, but knowing this thing had to be done. So I groaned and did what they said – I isolated the phones one by one. It looked as if the trouble was with the phone in Joy's bedroom – which is the central phone in the house – and once I'd done that and isolated it, I discovered that I could finally make it work and make calls on it, provided I pressed the button for messages. A voice would come through saying, "You have no messages…" and then immediately this would be followed by a normal line, which meant I could dial out.

But even then, no one could dial in. I rang my daughter and said, "Ring me back on this phone, will you?" And nothing happened. She couldn't get through. Finally she rang me on our fax phone, and said, "No result, I just get an engaged signal."

When Joy came home, I told her what was happening, and I said, "Have we got a spare phone anywhere?" She said, "Yes there's an old one downstairs." So I said, "Let's bring it up and try it." And to our delight and relief, it worked.

Then, a bit later in the afternoon, I discovered that I wasn't able to get through to the Web. I thought "I bet this is something to do with all that messing about with the phone." So I looked in that other room, couldn't see anything wrong, except there was something unplugged, that didn't appear to be anything to do with the Web – just an extension to the answering machine. But I plugged it in, then went back to my computer, and sure enough, I was back on the Web.

It was then that I realised that all this struggle had put me in a thoroughly optimistic state of mind so that the tiredness didn't matter. I went on my walk bubbling with energy and feeling absolutely wide awake. I thought, "It's funny. Normally my tiredness is obviously an illusion. Just due to the fact that I think, 'God, I've been working bloody hard.' And since I've agreed to do this book on serial killers, a 130,000-word book in two months..." [*I laugh and he says:*] Yes, it's really heavy work. But what I'd just demonstrated to myself was the mechanism of false fatigue. If I say to myself: "My God. I've done three thousand words today," something inside me says, "Well you ought to be exhausted." And

30

instantly I feel exhausted. And you realise that it's your own mind playing tricks.

Anyway, I was talking about the problems of this book... About six months ago, a friend of mine called Herbie Brennan, who's quite a good fantasy writer, said that his latest book was doing very well with Bloomsbury, who publish Harry Potter. He said, "Why don't you try your *Spider World* on them?" And I thought, "Oh, what a good idea." So I wrote to his editor. The result was no reply. I tried again, and finally, her assistant wrote to say: "I'd love to see your fascinating novel *Spider World*." So I sent it along with great hopes.

Silence. Absolute silence. The silence goes on for month after month. Finally, I wrote and said, "What's happening?" And she said, "Oh sorry, I've been terribly busy, but I promise I'll get round to it soon." And then suddenly one day, the whole book came back, all four volumes of it, with a note saying, "Well, I'm sorry. Yes, I think this is a fascinating novel, but it's not for us." But not saying why. I mean, if you think a novel is fascinating and then turn it down, surely you ought to explain why.

I'd left the parcel unpacked. But a few days later, I wanted to send the book to a friend of mine. So I opened the parcel and looked at the books. It was obvious at a single glance that they'd never been opened. You could see, you know, the paperback, the fourth volume, was in mint condition. It had never been opened.

But after feeling irritable for a few minutes I realised once again that the same thing happened as with the rejection of the Angry Young Man book. That is, there was no sinking feeling, no sense of vulnerability, what Sartre called contingency. It was not affecting me in the least little bit. I was totally unaffected by it. And in a funny way, that pleased me as much as if the book had been accepted. There was that feeling of "It's taken you a lifetime, but you're gradually getting there."

BS: Well it was interesting what you said about getting on top of the problem as well, as with the review of the autobiography, by saying, "Well, they're wrong."

CW: Yes. I knew as I wrote it, objectively speaking, that this is a damn good book. And when you've written a hundred books, you know when it's good and when it's not.

BS: You must have used your journals a lot to write the autobiography.

CW: And letters. Dozens of letters I'd written to my family. My daughter Sally spent weeks sorting them out.

BS: How long did it take to do the book?

CW: A very short time, about three months. Because once I'd got the letters and all the rest of it, and settled down to writing, it was quite easy to do. Not like this Angry Young Man book, which is like climbing Everest in slippery shoes.

BS: I don't think I've ever read the first book of autobiography you did in the early 1960s.

CW: Just as well, because I used big chunks out of that in this new one. That was necessary because I'd totally forgotten them. Your memory for distant events just goes.

BS: It's amazing how you can forget... I tried writing an autobiography in my mid twenties, and then again last year. I never looked at the original while writing the recent one, but once I'd finished it I went back to the original and found I had forgotten so much of what had happened to me in my own life at the time!

CW: Absolutely. Goethe once advised someone: "Write your autobiography when you're young because you'll have forgotten half of it by the time you're forty." And in fact, he made the mistake of waiting until he was sixty, and the result is that *Poetry and Truth*, while a great book, is a dead book. It doesn't have the sort of sparkle that it would have contained if he'd written it when he was twenty-five.

BS: On the other hand, I wrote about the exact same period at twenty-five as at forty-six. And I did it on purpose the first time when young in order to have a photographic effect, but later in life I hoped to have a better intellectual view of things back then, a better view of who I was. And I think one can... Spender wrote his autobiography at about fifty – no, wait, forty.

CW: *World Within World?*

BS: Yes. I think he was about forty when he wrote it – or between forty and forty...

CW: No, Stephen was younger than that, because I knew him when he was forty. He was about that age when *The Outsider* came out, and Stephen was born, let's see, I think it was 1913, or somewhere about there. And *The Outsider* came out in 1956. Now I had read *World Within World* when I was nineteen or twenty, five years before.

BS: Maybe my idea of forty is that maybe it came out in 1949 or so.*

* Spender was born in February 1909 and *World Within World* was published in 1951

33

CW: That's right, yes, yes.

BS: That was a good book, that was an interesting book.

CW: Oh yeah. I thought it was a very interesting book. And I was about to write to Stephen at that time – I'm glad I didn't, in a way, because I'd done nothing – and just say how good I thought it was.

But that business about forgetting what you've done… it's tremendously important to write things down early. And the same way, I keep a taped journal, that will run into millions and millions of words, because I've been doing it since about 1980. Before that, I kept a written journal, which had already extended to millions of words.

BS: That is one of the good things about the autobiography. I thought there were several things that made it interesting. One is the re-creation of all the periods of your life. It makes you feel like you're there. And I think few people go to those pains to recreate that much with original notes and whatnot. And the other interesting thing is how your philosophy comes through the book as well. So it's a book that is not only a story, but it's also making a point, or teaching. Incidentally, I read that book, the defence of it…

CW: Meadley?

BS: Yes. You've read it?

CW: Of course, he sent it to me. But where did you get it?

BS: On the Internet, as a PDF file. This was after I read the autobiography. You had mentioned that it had bad reviews. So once I read it I searched the Internet to see what I could find. I looked for the bad reviews and I found this PDF at the Web site. They printed the book, I assume.

CW: No. I don't think it ever was printed.

BS: Ah, OK. So they made the PDF available.

CW: Robert Meadley, who prefers to be called Phil, is an interesting chap. A remarkable intellectual, a man of wide reading, yet he prefers to make a living as a plumber, just to give himself freedom. He's exactly what I mean by an Outsider. And that's also true of his publisher...

BS: Savoy?

CW: Savoy, yes. [*He corrects my pronunciation, as I put the accent on the first syllable, and he on the second.*] And Savoy started by saying they'd like to publish it, but I don't think they ever got around to that.

BS: Well I think the book was available on their site.

CW: Oh.

BS: It was fun reading, although he gets pretty obscure and bizarre with his style at times.

CW: Yes. Well, the one thing I'm glad he wrote that for is that bit about Humphrey Carpenter. I was very glad to see that. Because Carpenter really – he's dead now – stabbed me in the back. He came to see me here, saying, "I'd like to write about you, can I come and meet you?" "Do you mind if I call you Colin?" And soon his emails began "My dear Colin." He seemed quite a decent sort, and Joy found him charming. His father was the Bishop of Oxford. But I was a bit puzzled when he sent me the typescript of his book only a few weeks after coming to see me – I didn't realise it had reached that stage, and he took care not to tell me, otherwise I'd have smelled a rat. I read his introductory chapter, describing his visit to see me, and thought it was rather snide, but not too bad. Then the proof came, and I glanced at the Introduction, just to make sure he'd added the corrections I'd asked for – such as calling this house a cottage. Then Joy said "Have you read his chapter about you?" and I said "No" – I don't like reading about myself. So she said "Read it," and I did. And it turned out to be a sneering attack on me, dismissing me as a one-book writer.

BS: And he finished it all like two weeks later… he hadn't even used the visit really?

CW: Yes, absolutely. He came here in order to be able to use it in the first chapter, so he could say he'd interviewed at least one of the Angry Young Men. I felt it was about as filthy a trick as ever has been played on me.

BS: Well, I looked into him as well. I knew his name but I didn't know anything about him. So I did a search and found an obituary about him which said he was "a man of intense kindness… with an absolute lack of malice." And I thought, what is this?

CW: In a sense, I don't blame him. It was weakness and stupidity more than malice. He'd churned out the book to make money, and had used reviews and articles written in the '50s. And since he was pretty brainless, he wouldn't have understood what I had to say about Husserl and Sartre. He actually fell asleep on the settee while I was talking to him as I am to you, about ideas. When I read his book I understood why. Talking to him about phenomenology was a sure way of putting him to sleep. [Laughs]

BS: It's very strange. It's strange because I know you have many fans and admirers, but who don't have the power to do a book…

CW: Yes. Fortunately, I seem to have become a cult figure, and so I don't get into the state in which I think – as one might be tempted to at my age – "Oh my God I've been working for all these years and I'm still unknown…" Because you know…

BS: It's funny, I have spoken to some of the young people who come to work at the Herald Tribune sometimes from England who haven't heard of you. And I'm very surprised. But then others have heard…

CW: Well don't forget that the culture has changed so completely since *The Outsider* came out. I don't understand all the changes that have taken place since then. For example in the '90s there was a group of writers in London who launched a magazine called the Modern Review, and were regarded as the Young Turks of modern literature. They were Post-*Martin* Amis [*Laughs and puts emphasis on Martin*] and all that.

BS: Post-*Martin* Amis…

CW: Post-Martin Amis, yes.

BS: And then there's the Granta crowd. This woman who attacked you in an interview did a story in Granta. I looked into all these reviews of yours after reading the book. And I found this one by this woman.

CW: In The Observer.

BS: I thought it ran in The Sunday Times…

CW: No, The Observer. The chap who did the other piece in The Sunday Times who came to interview me was actually a very nice fellow, who did a nice, but rather boring sort of interview.

BS: Well this woman, it was quite interesting – you know who I'm talking about?

CW: Lynn Barber.

BS: That's right. I did a search on her and discovered that she had a story printed in Granta about how she'd been seduced by a conman when she was sixteen – he was much older than her and was married and had children, but she didn't know this. Her parents even apparently approved him before they knew the truth – with the result that she had ever after mistrusted people, feeling betrayed even by her parents. It seems to have been traumatic. She said it taught her that everyone is capable of living a lie and she said that it was a good lesson for her interviews, but not for life. I thought it was an interesting background to the story she did on you.

CW: Yes, it is. She also did a piece about a friend of mine, Richard Adams, who wrote *Watership Down*, which was so vicious that it must have made his eyes water. But Richard is enthusiastic about sex and talks a lot about it. I mentioned in the autobiography that I said to Richard, "When I was sixteen I wanted to fuck every girl in the world." And Richard said, "I still do."

BS: I thought you were going to say he had…

CW: Anyway, this could be why Lynn Barber took agin him. But in my case, you know, I don't quite know why she got the razor out. Of course, I was fairly open and frank with her, as I normally am. And I said "I've always enjoyed making love to Joy. It's one of the greatest pleasures of my life."

BS: And she had mentioned negatively, I thought, about Joy coming through and saying she'd put out the dustbin bags, or something like that. Her approach was obviously, "The poor woman is a slave," or something.

CW: Oh, well, it didn't worry me and, oddly enough, I don't feel terribly upset about her. It was fair enough. I knew beforehand that she was that type of person and was going to do a rather negative piece. And she could have been much more negative, believe it or not. I must go and have a pee. [*While walking out of the room:*] I don't really object to Lynn Barber. It's people like Humphrey Carpenter I object to, who drive the knife in between your shoulder blades, when they've held out a friendly hand.

[*End of the first tape*]

The Interview: Two

BRAD SPURGEON: Moving on now to your fiction. I enjoyed the chess bit in *The Personality Surgeon*.

COLIN WILSON: That's a good book, isn't it? I enjoyed writing that.

BS: Do you play chess?

CW: No. You don't have time I think if you're a writer to do this kind of thing. It requires too much focused energy. No major writer has ever been good at anything but writing. Languages, for instance. No writer can ever be bothered to speak more than his own language. People who are good at languages are always minor writers.

BS: Hmm. That's interesting. And you think writers can't play chess because...

CW: They don't have time to. You can only do one thing really well. And if you try doing more than one thing well, you're just dissipating your energies.

BS: Well Conrad... Conrad... languages, I suppose you're talking about several languages... because Conrad wrote in his second... you know, he wrote in English...

CW: Oh yes, certainly. But I have to admit I don't like Conrad at all. He's a gloomy bastard. I can't read him. Undoubtedly a major writer, but his pessimism and self-pity irritate the hell out of me. He's another one like Camus. One of these people who sees the world as a pretty lousy place.

BS: It's very important for you as a reader and critic, what the point of view is, as opposed to simply the beauty of the writing, isn't it?

CW: Yes, I can enjoy a writer like Henry James, who is basically in some ways rather negative about life – although I think his brother was a far greater writer and a far greater intellect – but on the other hand I can enjoy James simply because he had such a good mind. And I appreciate a good mind. TS Eliot said he was the most intelligent man of his time.

BS: Well that's one of the things I really enjoy about your fiction. I've read so much uninteresting fiction for so long that... it goes in waves of what one reads I suppose, and maybe I got into a trough of reading uninteresting stuff... but I'm sorry to say that although you were one of my favourite writers I had never read your fiction.

CW: Oh. [*Slight sound of alarm.*]

BS: I had read most of the crime books, all the occult books, *The Outsider*, and other Outsider cycle books

42

and I think I had a prejudice. I did own one of the novels, which I think was *The Philosopher's Stone*, and at one point I read the first page and that was it. But I would go back to it now after I have read some of your others. I think possibly my prejudice was that I liked your non-fiction so much that I thought I could not like your fiction, that you could not be a good fiction writer. But for this interview, I thought I'd better read some of the fiction, and that's why I asked you for suggestions. I read them in the order they were written. I first read *The Mind Parasites*, then *The Personality Surgeon* and I've started *Spider World* but haven't had the time to finish it…

CW: That's probably my masterpiece.

BS: *Spider World?*

CW: Oh yeah.

BS: I've noticed already that it is the most… but I haven't read that much – but it seems that as a fiction writer you are at a level that you weren't at in the other books…

CW: Yes.

BS: The control and the…

CW: Well I found I just took off. And I suddenly discovered that, if you know what I mean, the book was writing me.

BS: That's why I wanted to read it, because you said that in the autobiography. I have seen that there has been a progress in the fiction writing… But to go back to the point: the intellectual side. So few fiction writers today make use of the intellect, or if they do it's an intelligence that's not the most interesting kind to me. And I think the extraordinary thing in both

43

of these books, *The Mind Parasites* and *The Personality Surgeon*, is that there's an intellectual story. Although the intellectual bit in *The Mind Parasites* is much more bookish than in *The Personality Surgeon*. What I found interesting is how you are the same writer doing the non-fiction as the fiction, you're using fiction to say the same things, and it's just as compelling.

CW: Thank you.

BS: Incidentally I also read many years ago your book about writing fiction.

CW: *The Craft of the Novel*.

BS: But I wonder, perhaps do you have readers that read the fiction but don't read the non-fiction?

CW: I don't know. Some people I know prefer the fiction.

BS: Has it ever been a problem as a writer to be writing so many different kinds of non-fiction and fiction…

CW: No, I always believed that this was necessary. Shaw talked about the artist/philosopher, and I discovered from the beginning that this is what I felt I was. And don't forget I was writing fiction long before I was writing non-fiction. I had been writing *Ritual in the Dark* since I was sixteen, and long before *The Outsider*. In fact, *The Outsider* was a kind of an offshoot of *Ritual*. So when I was twenty I thought of myself as a novelist.

BS: You can see the progression of the fiction writing, which is not to say there is anything wrong with *The Mind Parasites*, for instance, but it seems to me you now have more of a sense of drama amongst more characters, a larger canvas. Dramatize, dramatize. Who said that?

CW: Henry James.

BS: It is interesting to me also about how the Angry Young Man thing was a creation of the press and you weren't really an angry young man.

CW: Not at all. You see, some people, like John Osborne, quite enjoyed being called Angry Young Men. Because it gave him an identity. And the result was that he got a number plate for his car, AYM1. But I wasn't angry about anything. Why should I be? I'm basically a thinker. I'm not going to jump up and down and shout – that would amount to being carried away by negative emotion, and negative emotion disgusts me.

BS: And in fact it was beneficial to begin with to have had this massive success, but then afterwards that had a negative, a downside to it, as well.

CW: What it made me do, was, once again, go back to being the outsider. In my early life I was really forced to learn to be independent and not to get upset and miserable about setbacks. Because, you know, I really did have to pull my cart out of the mud. And then *The Outsider* came out and I thought, "My God, I was quite wrong." I was expecting it to be violently attacked, and get the same kind of reception that Nietzsche got for *The Birth of Tragedy*, and instead here were people saying I was a genius.

By the time the second book came out, *Religion and the Rebel*, I'd had over a year of silly non-stop publicity, and the horsewhipping scandal when Joy's family turned up at my flat, and her father shouted "Wilson, the game is up", and told Joy I was a homosexual and had six mistresses. That hit all the front pages. And we then made the mistake of fleeing to Dublin, pursued by the Daily Express, and the story broke in Time Magazine. That was when my publisher said, "For God's sake get out of London, or you'll never write another book." Which is why we moved down here, to Cornwall. And my sequel to *The Outsider* came out six months later. You can see why no one took it seriously. It got slaughtered. Yes, in a sense I felt oddly relieved. I was sick of being in the spotlight, sick of standing on a pedestal. So it was a relief to have my feet back on the ground. Becoming famous was really pretty bloody. It was like that odd feeling you get when you've had slightly too much to drink, and feeling woozy so the room goes round. And you're rushing from party to party and interview to interview and television studio to television studio. So it was quite a relief in a way and to feel, "OK now, let's get down to living like a writer and doing some serious work." Because even when everybody was attacking me, I never had any doubt that what I've got to do is important. I knew this from the beginning, when I was in my teens – that I've got something extremely important to do.

BS: How well do you feel you've succeeded?

CW: Oh, I think I've succeeded totally. What I'm saying hasn't been understood yet. But there's plenty of time. I'll be dead for a long time…

BS: There are writers like Truman Capote who got so used to his celebrity status that that was all he did after that, was to be a celebrity.

CW: It destroyed him. But also, of course, he went onto drugs and alcohol and so on.

BS: It probably goes together… he wasn't using his brain or his talent…

CW: Unfortunately. I don't object to Truman Capote, although he did make some nasty remarks about me once. But basically I quite admire him, even though he didn't have anything tremendously important to say. And he was full of emotions and feelings – he lived on an emotional switchback. I'm not saying it's because he was homosexual, either. There have been plenty of homosexuals I have liked very much indeed, Stephen Spender, WH Auden, Chris Isherwood...

BS: Angus Wilson.

CW: Certainly Angus. And Sandy Wilson. But basically I don't like this kind of temperament of people like Capote, who get terribly personal and bitchy.

BS: Like this other guy who attacked the autobiography, I think...

CW: In The Observer.

BS: Adam... Mars-Jones.

CW: Mars-Jones, yes, really vicious.

BS: Incidentally, one of my English teachers at university did a bibliography of Angus Wilson's books, and knew him quite well, and I had a very funny experience in the mid-eighties. I was working in the library of the Herald Tribune and I had just heard from that English teacher that Angus Wilson had moved to France. I opened up the *Who's Who* and looked for Wilson, and saw that he lived in St-Rémy-de-Provence. The address was a post box, #180, or something. The next day I was again at work and dealing with the mail inquiries from the readers of the newspaper addressed to the library. I picked up a letter sent in France and looked at the back of it and the address said, Boite Postale, #180, St-Remy-de-Provence. I recognised it instantly as the same address as Angus Wilson. I didn't know anything about Wilson's personal life, but when I opened the letter I found it was written by someone who signed it not Angus Wilson, but Tony Garrett.

CW: Oh! Yes.

BS: But to me the name was a very Dickensian sounding name. I thought of the writer in his garret. So I said to myself, "This is a made up name." Wilson does not want to be recognised by whoever might open his mail at the newspaper – although I thought that a bit odd. In any case, the letter writer wanted to have a copy of a small article we had published about a change to inheritance laws in France. [*Wilson and Garrett – who I later learned was his life-long companion – had made the mistake of moving to France just before it became clear that Angus was getting permanently ill*] So I sent him the story that we ran and I wrote a letter with it. In the letter I said that I had surmised that the writer was either Angus Wilson or someone close to him, as I knew this was his address. I mentioned the coincidence of how I knew this, having that English professor who was a mutual friend and having checked the *Who's Who* the day before the letter arrived. So, Tony Garrett responded, sending me a copy of Wilson's most recent book, signed for me. And he wrote me a letter telling me about the problem Angus had with his mind slipping. In your book you gave the illness a different name than what I thought it was. I thought it was Alzheimer's.*

*Angus Wilson suffered from hydro-encephalitis, which has Alzheimer's like symptoms

CW: Something like that, yes, I can't remember exactly what it was. It was a terribly pity, really, because I'm sure that Angus's decline and death were due to the fact that, a bit like Truman Capote, he got too fond of the high life of the writer, rushing from committee to committee and lecturing non-stop. It's terribly important, if you're a writer, to get *away* from people, move *quietly* to the country and get on with your work. It's enormously important.

BS: The other thing I found interesting in reading *The Mind Parasites*, was that I thought that your interest in the occult came much later, but when you read *The Mind Parasites* you see that all the basis, the grounds for a belief in the occult, were already there.

CW: Oh certainly. I had been interested in that kind of thing for a long time. Almost always, as you see from the autobiography. But I didn't take a terribly serious interest in it to begin with. I was pretty certain of the existence, let's say, of ghosts. For example, there is a piece in a novel of mine called *The World of Violence*, describing a ghost that Bill Hopkins* had seen down in their cottage. The old gardener, who was dead, used to appear raking leaves at the end of the garden. It struck me as odd, you know, very curious.

BS: You must have had a predisposition to changing your scientific… instinct…

CW: Orientation, yes. I certainly did, but then again, my interest, that feeling that science was the be-all

*One of the 'Angry Young Men' and personal friend of Colin Wilson whose novel of philosophical ideas, *The Divine and the Decay*, was a succes de scandale (MacGibbon & Kee, 1957)

and end-all went out of the window with my nihilistic period in my teens because it was quite obvious that science could not answer the basic questions. Even, "Where does space end?" And once I'd started to think about this question of "why we're here" and "what are we supposed to do now we're here", I remembered that Dostoyevsky once said, "If there really is life after death, it's the most important thing we can possibly know." Yet while I agreed with this in the abstract, I couldn't feel this provided an answer. Because even if there's life after death, that wouldn't be an answer to why we're alive. My feeling was, "While we're here on this earth, our business is to concentrate on why we're alive, not on life after death."

In fact, it's only in recent years that I have become absolutely, totally convinced about life after death. When I'd written *The Occult* in 1970, I'd been impressed by the evidence, but not totally convinced. It wasn't until 1985, when I was asked to write a book called *Afterlife* that I saw that the evidence is overwhelming. Yet being convinced by evidence provided by other people still left me with a touch of scepticism. An existentialist wants to see and touch the answer. It's rather like a judge in a murder case saying: "I agree the circumstantial evidence is overwhelming, but I don't like to condemn a man to death on circumstantial evidence – can't you offer anything more concrete?" Existentialism is a desire for concrete evidence.

Over the years I'd become friendly with a member of the Society for Psychical Research called Montague Keen. Perhaps his most important work concerned a small group who held séances in the cellar of a farmhouse at Scole, in Norfolk. They were obtaining some of the most convincing phenomena in the history of psychical research, so convincing that the possibility of fraud was virtually nil.

The last time I bumped into Monty was at a conference in London in November 2003. He had just married a new wife called Veronica, a friendly little Irishwoman. A few months later I heard that Monty had dropped dead of a heart attack. Then one day, Veronica rang me, and told me that ever since his death, Monty had been constantly in touch with her – she was even aware of his presence in bed. She'd be sitting up reading in the middle of the night, and the phone would ring, and a voice would say, "You don't know me, but I'm a medium and live in Ireland. I've got your husband here and he said it's OK to ring you up because you're sitting in bed reading." And then he would deliver some absolutely spot-on message that couldn't be from anyone but Monty.

Veronica has started the Montague Keen Foundation, and I've agreed to write a book about him. I shall call it *The Return of Monty Keen.*

In *Afterlife* there's a chapter called 'Invasion of the Spirit People', which happened in 1847 when banging noises started in a cottage belonging to the Fox family in New York State. They called in the neighbours, and one of them asked aloud whether it was a spirit, and to give one rap for yes and two for no, and one rap sounded loud and clear. Then, using a code of raps, it said it was a peddler who had been murdered in the cellar for his money. Years later, the cellar was excavated, and they found a skeleton, and a peddler's box.

In no time, everybody in America was playing this game of communication with the dead, and the first Spiritualist church was founded.

So spiritualism took off and it never looked back. About twenty years later, the Society for Psychical Research was started, made up mainly of non-believers who simply wanted to get at the truth and find out if it was all a fraud. And although they never achieved their aim – proving life after death with scientific certainty – they at least left no doubt that it wasn't just fakery.

And yet although I had never doubted that it was genuine, it never interested me terribly. I'd always got more practical things to do than go to séances.

When Veronica asked me to write a book about Monty, Joy wasn't too keen – she was afraid I'd get a reputation like Conan Doyle, regarded as a spiritualist crank. And I also realise that it could be a dubious kind of thing to get mixed up in, because I've never wanted to get mixed up in spiritualism. Not really because I don't believe in it, but because I think it is irrelevant to my real concerns, which are philosophy and human evolution. And I wouldn't like to get a reputation like Conan Doyle.

BS: I was going to ask… in some sense, you might be considered to be in a line, a tradition here….

CW: Certainly. There have been plenty of philosophers who've taken it seriously – William James, Henry Bergson, Hans Driesch, CD Broad. But the trouble with Conan Doyle was that not only did he become an enthusiastic spiritualist, but he stopped writing good books. He didn't write another *Lost World* or *Hound of the Baskervilles* after he became a spiritualist.

BS: That would be a concern of yours?

CW: Ohh… sure. [A *little surprised*] Because it seems to me that writing books and getting down ideas is far more important. But I do, as I get older, have a very strong feeling that life has a meaning and purpose. In fact, it seems to me to be self-evidently meaningful. That's why I get so irritable about Sartre with his "Man is a useless passion." What's more, the meaning is somehow inherent in the very fabric of the act of living. And we can get through to it by a particular kind of focus, a particular kind of concentration. And if we could actually learn to get through to this, we would produce a new kind of human being – somebody with an enormous mental energy, who would be practically undefeatable.

It seems obvious to me that the human race has met so many setbacks that they are far too defeat-prone. It's more true now than ever before, because our technological world has separated us from our roots. Well, I think we're going back to the roots. I think that human beings will, sometime during the next century, be transformed. There's going to be a different kind of human being. And what will happen is that they'll create this peculiar ability that I'm talking of, of being able to remain in touch with reality all the time. The peak experience, for example, will be the easiest thing in the world to create. The Hindu saint Ramakrishna could plunge into Samadhi whenever he liked.

BS: It would be nice; because mostly what we've seen in history is repetition… human nature hasn't changed.

CW: No, not at all. We've now reached a point where it's absolutely urgent for something to happen.

Buckminster Fuller said, "I seem to be a verb." And when you're in these states of certainty, non-robotic states, this is what happens. You become a verb. And when human beings can learn to put themselves into that state in which they become a verb, then everything's going to change.

William James said in his essay 'The Energies of Men' that men have all kinds of hidden powers inside themselves which they never use.* We are all in the same state as a neurasthenic patient (that's the word they used then to describe nervous exhaustion) – the only difference being that such a person is ill, and we are not ill. The trouble is simply a habit of inferiority to our full selves.

BS: That goes back to one of your other ideas that I find interesting, which is the self-image idea – that if we see ourselves in a better way we can do more what we want to do, be more fulfilled. As I was growing up I was seen a little as the dummy of my family, I was the idiot of the three children, I was very bad in school – particularly in high school – and everybody thought I was only good for working in a circus – which is what I did end up doing at first. But I discovered slowly that I had a brain... and then I became intellectual and went to university, late, three or four years later than the other kids my age. But it was self-image as well. I saw myself the way other people saw me. I accepted it. Until I decided not to accept it and then they had to accept what they saw.

CW: Absolutely. It's the recognition that it's the way

*See Appendix 2

people *see themselves* that determines what they think they can achieve. *We* don't realise how much strength we have. That we're verbs. As Mr Polly said, "If you don't like your life, you can change it." And it really is amazing that as soon as you actually settle down to trying to change your life, and recognise that you are a verb, things begin to happen. Odd synchronicities happen. You know when you're in a good physical state and spiritual state because synchronicities start happening. I've noticed this again and again and again. You'll recall I describe it in the autobiography – how, for example, just as I finished my book on UFOs, which contains a lot about synchronicity, I woke up wondering what the time was, and thought, as I turned over in bed: "I bet it's 4:44," and sure enough it was 4:44.

BS: I have a strong sense of time like that…

CW: But this kind of synchronicity had been happening all the time as I was writing the last chapters of that book: 1:11, 2:22, 3:33. Again and again. Preposterous, thousands of times more than chance.

BS: Incidentally, racing drivers have peak experiences and heightened awareness while driving. There was even one, Ayrton Senna, a three-time world champion and considered to be one of the finest ever, who actually had out-of-body experiences while driving. He had one particular experience he spoke of in Monaco during a qualifying lap in 1988. His teammate, Alain Prost, had just set a lap time that no one thought could be beaten. Senna then beat it – with the same equipment, the same team's car – by nearly a second and a half, which is massive. And he spoke of how he went to this different level of existence, and he found

55

himself actually peering at the car on the track below him, the track having become like a tunnel. He felt he was above the car and watching himself drive it. Extraordinary… at high speed around this narrow, dangerous track through the city streets of Monaco. He was a somewhat mystical kind of person. And he got killed eventually, because when the car didn't have it, he tried to make up for whatever it did not have, and he just went too far.*

CW: Oh dear. That's sad.

BS: But back to the fiction again, you know, I liked the end of *The Personality Surgeon*. Suddenly Colin Wilson appears. That was highly unexpected.

CW: Oh! Good, I'm glad you did. I'm delighted, because I myself had tremendous difficulty finishing that book, until Don Seaman, the friend I used to walk with every day, suggested that ending, about the psychological profiling of killers, and I saw immediately: Yes, that's the answer.

BS: It's true the book climbs up like this, steadily, and getting close to the end, I said, "How is he going to wrap this all up?" And I thought that was quite effective… Because also, if one knows the author, and

---

*Of the experience at Monaco Senna said, "At that moment, I suddenly realised that I was going beyond the threshold of consciousness." He would later say, "On a given day, a given circumstance, you think you have a limit and you go for this limit and you touch this limit and you think, OK, this is the limit. As soon as you touch this limit, something happens and you realise that you can suddenly go a little bit further. With your mind power, your determination, your instinct, and your experience as well, you can fly very high." Senna died at thirty-four on 1 May 1994 at the San Marino Grand Prix at Imola, while leading the race in a car that was not intrinsically as fast as that of the driver behind him, Michael Schumacher.

Colin Wilson's interests and whatnot, you can see your ideas in the book... but then you suddenly materialize. It's not just a game; Colin Wilson is not going to hide behind this narrative.

CW: Good, because Frank DeMarco, the publisher who has done quite a few of my books, would have liked to re-publish *The Personality Surgeon* but didn't like the ending and wanted me to re-write it. And I brooded on it but I couldn't think of any better ending.

BS: In some ways, it seems your life has gone in a circle. Do you think your life has gone in a circle, you've come back around? You had great success in the beginning, then the critics ridiculed you, and then you had success again with *The Occult* in the early 1970s and critical acclaim again. And just when one would have thought you would have had more, you've suddenly had these attacks on the autobiography. But in a way I would say it is similar to the beginning... is it going in circles?

CW: I don't really know. All I can tell you is that all that early success convinced me that success is danger-ous. Too much success gets you resting on your laurels and creates a kind of quicksand that you can't get out of. So I was relieved to get away from London and come down here and settle down to work. I'm a workaholic by temperament. I think it keeps you psychologically healthy.

I've often said to Joy, "I can't think of any worse fate than being enormously successful, say like Andrew Lloyd Webber." It must be dreadful to be as successful as that. There's nowhere to go. Now all I would have wanted to be highly successful for is to make enough money to be able to live comfortably. And you know,

we live more or less comfortably, so I've no particular reason to want that – we're nearly always broke…
[*Laughs*]

BS: I was amazed at discovering that in the autobiography, how you lived with a massive overdraft for so many years. To live in that way, with that pressure. Although at the same time, I suppose you're just living on an advance all the time.

CW: That's right. Yes. And in the same way, those panic attacks, which seemed to me at the time to be entirely bad. I'd wake up in the middle of the night and plunge into a state of depression, and my heart would begin pounding so that I was afraid it would explode. Of course, that scares you, and that makes it beat harder still. It's a feeling of vulnerability, like walking across a frozen pond and the ice suddenly giving way. So understandably, I couldn't see any possible good in them whatsoever; I realised later that in fact they were an essential step on the way to getting beyond them. And I came to realise that it was a benevolent fate that put me through them.

BS: You say you're not reading much fiction these days. Are there any fiction writers you do like?

CW: Well the only one I've discovered in recent years is Philip Pullman. A friend of mine, John Pick, who is an expert on David Lindsay, the author of *A Voyage to Arcturus*, told me about his trilogy, because John thought he'd been influenced by David Lindsay. Have you read Pullman's book?

BS: No I haven't.

CW: It's an amazing thing called, *His Dark Materials* – a three-volume novel. So I got it, and thought, "My

God, this is good." I dropped him a line, and said how much I admired it. And I was delighted when he said he'd been enthusiastic about *Spider World*.

BS: I have heard of him. I must look at that. You mentioned Philip Roth's *Portnoy's Complaint*. Have you read his more recent stuff?

CW: No, no. I just wouldn't want to. I don't want to get all mixed up in Jewish neuroses.

BS: *The Human Stain* is quite amazing, actually. Very broad canvas.

CW: Well, if you recommend it, I'll read it. [*Said with the tone of: "if I really must"*]

BS: ...although I don't think I read it trying to keep in mind whether he was optimistic or pessimistic.

CW: Well, neither would I. But if I do find that a writer's cast of mind is pessimistic, and there is no compensation for the gloom, then I don't really see why I should plough on with it.

> [*He leaves again for another pee, as we had been drinking a little – although his is tea rather than the wine I have. He returns and we talk briefly about the mini-CD recording device that has been used for the interview, with its digital quality sound, which I say is particularly good for capturing interviews at the Formula One races where I cover the sport*]

BS: I noticed with your fiction, particularly *The Mind Parasites*, on the one hand it read like a complete fantasy, but on the other hand it read like a fable, or a symbol. You could read it in two ways. You could read it in the literal way, as science fiction, but you could also read it as allegory.

CW: If you asked me, what is the basis of all my work, particularly my early work, it's the feeling there's something basically wrong with human beings, and to try and put my finger on what it is. In *The Outsider* I called it original sin. But later on I said that the problem is that human beings are like grandfather clocks driven by watch springs. And I've tried to find all kinds of images to express that, which expresses the fact that our powers appear to be taken away from us by something, and *The Mind Parasites* was the perfect parable.

BS: Yes, it was a parable, wasn't it? You could read it both ways, as a science fiction story or as a parable. I imagine it could appeal to some people on just the basic level of science fiction, a fantastic tale.

CW: It was intended basically as a kind of parable.

BS: On another subject, I think you've had a problem that in North America we don't have as much of, which is the class problem in this country. I think Robert Meadley pointed this out, also.

CW: Yes.

BS: That there is some resistance in the literary establishment to somebody who is an intellectual who has come up and done it on his own and come from the working class...

CW: That is partially true. I mention that in this Angry Young Man book, citing chapter and verse – there is actually a sort of hostility. But you see, I've never been aware of the class problem myself. Unlike DH Lawrence, I've never given a fuck about my background or social status. It seemed to me that ideas were all that mattered. Class seemed to me no more significant to a writer than to a mathematician. And so I've always been singularly indifferent to the class issue. I've never felt, for example, working class, as John Braine and John Osborne and Alan Sillitoe did.

BS: A lot of people who didn't go to university often regret it and feel inferior throughout their lives. I was out of school for three or four years. I decided not to go to university – back to that bit about being the dummy of the family. Unlike you, I had the opportunity and decided not to, which was a bit foolish – not that I came from a rich family. So I kind of grew up in the first part of life thinking I wasn't going to be educated, and then discovered I was interested in books. And I discovered all of that before I went to university and as a result went to university. Yet, frankly, the books that influenced my life most were not the ones I read in university. But has it ever bothered you?

CW: No. In fact, I feel I was terribly lucky not to have gone to university because as it was I was pretty good at teaching myself, which is the only way you really learn anything. Besides, I was so fascinated by all the kinds of subjects – literature, philosophy, poetry, science – that it would have been hard to find a university that would let me do them all.

For example, I became fascinated by art in my late teens, and the result was that by the time I was twenty-five I knew as much about art as if I'd gone to the Courtauld Institute. Simply because I've always had a frantic desire to absorb knowledge. That's the urge that has driven me all my life.

BS: It's obvious that you came out ahead. University could have been quite a waste of time.

CW: I think so, yes. Iris Murdoch had this idea that I ought to go to university and offered to try and get me into Oxford. I said, "What for?" It seemed pointless. Someone asked the scholar Porson – who didn't have a university degree – why didn't he do a degree. And Porson said, "But who would examine me?"

BS: I felt I had to unlearn much of what I learned at university. I was interested in writing. And university was the last place to go to learn how to write.

CW: Mmm. I suppose I've been to university since, but to teach. [*Laughs*]

BS: I didn't know about that whole part of your life with the lecturing. It was fascinating. And you started by speaking on Speaker's Corner in Hyde Park.

CW: Yes. That's where Shaw learned to speak.

BS: And it helped.

CW: Yes, but I'd always been good at public speaking at school. And so talking on Hyde Park didn't really polish me up all that much.

BS: It's interesting how you said you spoke off the cuff, as well. You didn't prepare your lectures.

CW: I've always been a fairly spontaneous speaker. See, usually, if I'm lecturing publicly, I know at any given point there are six different directions I could go in. Six different things I could move onto. And when I've moved on to whichever I've chosen, there are still another six, and so on. Unless I'm pretty tired, which does happen now and then. I once lectured in New York, with jet lag, and then my brain was dead. But nevertheless, I knew what I'd got to say. I said it with great clarity, and when I told a friend afterwards, "That was a lousy lecture, I was tired," he said, "No, it was one of the best lectures you've ever given."

BS: What are you working on now?

CW: A book on serial killers called *Manhunters*. Which is about how they get caught. And then I want to do another volume of *Spider World*, which I've been planning for years. I also want to write a novel with my son Damon – which I refer to as my 'Weinbaum novel', Stanley G Weinbaum, this writer of the 30s. So I have various things on my plate. I shall do the Angry Young Man book next.

BS: Have you found a publisher?

CW: Well not yet, but that doesn't matter. What tends to happen with me is that provided I want to do the book enough, then I find a publisher.

BS: That's something you want to publish next year...?

CW: It doesn't matter how long I leave it in a sense because there's so much of it that's already in the autobiography that I'd rather the autobiography was way behind me. It's the kind of book that ideally would come out five years after the autobiography.

BS: What is it that you'd want to say about the Angry Young Man thing?

CW: Quite simply, that most of them had rather tragic lives. Even those who were apparently successful – put successful in inverted commas – John Osborne, who became famous with *Look Back in Anger*, then went steadily downhill, until his last play was taken off because nobody was coming to see it.

BS: He also did an autobiography...

CW: Yes, two volumes. Then there's Kenneth Tynan,

who just went steadily downhill with too much booze and too many cigarettes, and was obsessed with spanking girl's bottoms, and ended up a wreck. Kingsley Amis, who became an alcoholic. John Wain, who fizzled out and ended on the breadline. Humphrey Carpenter subtitled his book 'A Comedy of the Fifties'. But it was more like a tragedy for most of them.

BS: And you'll presumably say why?

CW: Absolutely. Because they had nothing really essential to say, no line to follow. One of the few of that period I admire was Doris Lessing. She was with the rest of us in that volume called *Declaration*.* And Doris seems to me to be one of the very few who has remained interesting. This is because her interests have moved from political issues to human evolution – which, of course, is dear to my heart.

BS: It is a bit strange that you were grouped in with these people and nearly all the others had the dreary ending and you're going strong.

CW: Simply because I was the only one with anything to say.

BS: A more long-term kind of message...

CW: Yes. Somebody asked Faulkner what he thought of new writers like Norman Mailer, William Styron and Gore Vidal. He said, "They write good, but they got nuttin' to say."

BS: What was that wonderful critique of somebody... "He doesn't write, he types."

* A collection of political-literary essays written by the group of people that were known as part of the 'Angry Young Men' wave, and edited by Tom Maschler. Published in 1957

CW: No! Truman Capote said that of me.

BS: Did he?

CW: In the Paris Review interview, he dismissed Kerouac as 'just a typist', and then when they asked, "What about Colin Wilson?" he said, "Oh, another typist." [*Laughs*]

BS: I didn't realise also what I learned in your autobiography, that you had this meeting with George Plimpton* way back in the early 1950s.

CW: The odd thing about George is that we got on terribly well in Paris, and when *The Outsider* came out, I thought George would be delighted. When I was in Paris later with Joy soon after that, I called in at the offices of the Paris Review. George wasn't there, but I left a message asking George to get in touch. He never did. Years later, in New York, again I sent him another message, no reply.

I suspect that the success of *The Outsider* put him off, and he developed a 'thing' about me. And one or two people have been the same. Kingsley Amis was another. You recall that in the autobiography I tell how Amis and Wain came out on to a roof at a party, and Amis said, "Look, there's that bugger Wilson, I'm going to push him off the roof." Wain had to hold him back, and told me about it years later. Amis was really, in some way, worried about me.

But you were asking me about Angry Young Men. John Braine was another one who fizzled. The whole book will

* First editor of the Paris Review from its founding in 1953 until his death in 2003; actor and author of books of journalism. March 18th, 1927 – September 25th, 2003

be about people who fizzled. Tremendously sad.

BS: How many are still around?

CW: Alan Sillitoe. Doris is still around. Can't think of any others. Doris is eighty.

BS: If you did do an Angry Young Man book it would sort of be the last word on the Angry Young Man...

CW: Presumably.

BS: Are you doing anything special for the anniversary, or do you know of anything that's happening?

CW: No.

BS: In a way it was a totally unexpected, bizarre thing that occurred in your life, wasn't it? You intended to write books and then this press creation happened and was something that...

CW: Nothing to do with me at all. It had the favourable effect, I suppose, of making me famous, and enabling me to make a living by writing. But it had the very unfavourable effect of making people hostile. Shaw aroused the same kind of hostility because he got so much publicity. But it didn't matter to Shaw – he was rich by that time. I wasn't – I still had to make a living. But it wasn't just the publicity. I think they probably would have been hostile anyway, because I'm basically a writer of ideas, and the English aren't interested in ideas. The English, I'm afraid, are totally brainless. It isn't like that across the Channel. If you're a writer of ideas like Sartre or Foucault, or Derrida, then the French public know your name, whereas here in England, their equivalent in the world of philosophy wouldn't be known.

BS: And the press even got the story wrong and continues to do so, don't they? Like you weren't sleeping on Hampstead Heath while writing *The Outsider…*

CW: That's right, I was writing *Ritual In the Dark* when I was sleeping on Hampstead Heath.

But then you see, *Ritual* was really the basis of *The Outsider*. Because as you know, I was explaining *Ritual in the Dark* to Bill Hopkins one evening, and I said it's about three types of people: one of whom has great discipline of the intellect, but not of the body or the emotions, one of whom has great discipline of the emotions but not of the intellect or the body, one of whom has great discipline of the body but not of the intellect or the emotions. And I said that if you could somehow roll all three of them together into one person they make an extraordinary human being. But as it is they're all unbalanced. And it was in thinking about this that I began to see the outline of *The Outsider*. Nietzsche is the intellectual who has great discipline of the intellect but not of the emotions or the body, Van Gogh has discipline of the emotions but not of the intellect or the body, Nijinsky has discipline of the body but not of the emotions or the intellect. Then I realised this was also true of the three brothers Karamazov. So that was a centrally important idea.

BS: Have you done a lot of books that haven't been published?

CW: Not really, no. Although there's still a huge sequel to *The Space Vampires* that hasn't found a publisher.

BS: It took a long time for one of the volumes of *Spider World* to be published, didn't it?

CW: For the last volume to come out. And I only wrote the last one because this dear friend of mine, Frank DeMarco, who runs Hampton Roads in Virginia, said, would I like to write a fantasy novel? And I said, "Have you read *Spider World?*" And he said, "What's *Spider World?*" And I said, "Well, I think it's my best novel." So I sent him *Spider World* and he liked it, and asked me to write the unwritten fourth volume. Hampton Roads ended by publishing all four. And in due course I shall go on and write the fifth, which is called, *New Earth.*

BS: And how many do you project? Just the five?

CW: The fifth. I don't really see beyond that. But it'll be complete with the fifth. Whether the fifth will be in two parts like the others I don't know.

BS: The range of your fiction is amazing, and of your writing in general. You have these underlying ideas that surface everywhere. But there is a vast range. Is that something that you purposefully exercise at producing?

CW: Well, no, but I've always been interested in a variety of things. One of my main problems as far as the public is concerned is that I'm interested in too many things. I've written books on philosophy, on psychology, on occultism, on criminology, even on music and wine. And if the critics can't typecast you, I'm afraid you tend not to be understood. In the 1960s, a television producer from the BBC came to see me with the idea of making a programme about me. But after a weekend, he said "Sorry, it's impossible. I don't even know where to begin."

BS: We haven't talked about the crime writing. I can't imagine that it does your reputation or popularity that much good to associate with criminals like Ian Brady, to be known as somebody who has corresponded with him and done a preface to his book – I think – and encouraged him on that. But perhaps you don't care about that either…

CW: I've never worried in the least about my reputation. I've done whatever I've particularly wanted to do at the time.

But in any case, my interest in crime, I've always felt, was shared by Dostoyevsky and Balzac, and even Dickens. It's basically a psychological interest in crime and criminals. Dostoyevsky's best novel, I think, is a thing called *The House of the Dead*, which is more or less the realistic account of his period in the prison camp in Siberia and the criminals he met there.

Criminals have always interested me because for me, they are the obverse side of creativity. They're the obverse of the saint. And what's more, we spend so much of our time in a state of total indifference about meaning and morality that you only have to then read some book in which a stupid crime occurs, like Capote's *In Cold Blood*, to suddenly be awakened to a feeling of the importance of human decency.

A friend of mine, who was a headmaster, said that when he was at a grammar school one of the masters there claimed that there was no such thing as morality, that the word was completely meaningless. Nothing Hugh said could convince him otherwise. And then one day this master commented to him about another master: "I can't stand him, there's something evil about him." And Hugh said, "You mean that he doesn't conduce to the greatest good of the greatest number?" – Jeremy Bentham's definition of goodness – and he thought for a moment, then said "No, I don't." He had suddenly awakened to the fact that there were some matters of human behaviour in which he wasn't a materialist. Now whenever I write about crime, it has this same effect on me – makes me aware that there is such a thing as morality.

In the bootleg era there was an American gangster called Charlie Birger, who murdered dozens of people. But as he was standing on the scaffold, he said, "It *is* a beautiful world, isn't it." And then the trap dropped. Now, if he'd realised that earlier, he wouldn't have ended on the scaffold.

BS: I like your 'shortcut' theory, about how criminals do their crimes because they are seeking a shortcut to some thing. Having read the theory and then analysed crimes, you can link it up and see the truth of the theory.

CW: Yes, and that's something I realise again and again as I write this book about serial killers – that they're "fuck ups". You know, crime writers like to write about 'great criminals', a Vautrin or Professor Moriarty. But that's shit. Criminality is just a way of screwing up your life. None of them are any good. Their minds are too small. They're little more than children.

BS: Interesting because most popular fictional portrayals of so-called master-criminals is that the Moriarties are smart…

CW: Somebody asked Dennis Nielsen, the British serial killer, what he thought of Hannibal Lecter in *The Silence of the Lambs*, and he said, "Absolute fantasy. He's presented as tremendously potent… I've never felt potent in my life."

And this is the problem. What is interesting is the fantasy that crime, particularly sex crime, can give the criminal a glimpse of power, rather like a large whiskey. And that is why sex criminals do it. Ted Bundy, when he first started abducting girls in Seattle, took them up to Taylor Mountain and would spend the whole night raping them. He obviously felt that he was accessing a degree of sexual power that would never have been possible in his normal life. His girlfriend Meg Anders said he needed to truss her up with ropes before he could really enjoy sex. You can see that it's a quest for the feeling of potency.

And a chap I'm writing about at the moment, Mike DeBardeleben, who kidnapped one of his victims, took her back to his home and then proceeded to rape her for a full hour without reaching a climax, and he continued. Well, quite remarkable. The sexual Olympics. It was the sense of doing something forbidden that turned him into a sexual athlete.

Now this is perhaps the most important thing I have to say about crime and criminals – that no matter how much they indulge in self-justification, as Brady does, something deep inside them revolts against what they're doing, and drains their wellsprings of vitality. A journalist called Fred Harrison went to interview Brady in prison, and Brady admitted "I felt old at twenty six," and admitted that he was experiencing the 'Ecclesiastes effect', the feeling that nothing is worth doing. He said: "I had experienced everything." And the same thing happened to Leonard Lake, who must be the sickest murderer of all time – he lived in a remote house in California, lured women there by inviting them for a meal with their family, then murdered the husband and child and raped the woman for days before killing her. He had an accomplice called Charles Ng, and they videotaped their rapes. They got caught when Ng tried to steal a vice from a hardware store, and Lake killed himself with a cyanide capsule. And when the police went to search the farm, they found the videos, and Lake's diaries. And the diaries revealed that he'd also sunk into a state of boredom and self-disgust.

There's a law of the universe that says: "You can't achieve personal evolution by doing harm to other people. You just achieve your own piecemeal destruction."

Yet Brady, like the Marquis de Sade, believed that by total self-indulgence he'd achieve the ultimate peak experience. And it didn't work any better for Brady than it did for Sade or Leonard Lake.

There's a psychologist – Mihaly Csikszentmihalyi – who wrote a book called *The Flow Experience*, which became a best seller in the States. He discovered that the flow experience – that feeling of a smooth flow of energy – was common to athletes, writers, musicians, even members of motorcycle gangs. He had recognised that the flow experience gives you a sudden feeling of freedom, of genuine inner freedom. And as I was reading it, it dawned on me that sex maniacs like Bundy and DeBardeleben are the same. They're all seeking the flow experience.

BS: Which is like the peak experience…

CW: It *is* the peak experience… Mihaly Csikszentmihalyi says that you find it in a lot of people with whom you wouldn't want to associate the word peak experience, because you tend to associate that with fairly serious writers and thinkers. But it is the peak experience. Our vital forces are like a stream which is flowing across a flat plain and has gradually developed more and more twists and bends. And it gradually turns into a muddy trickle. But when someone like Bundy commits rape, it has the effect of a sudden rainstorm that sends a flood down the mountain, and all the river bends are swept away, and suddenly it flows deep and clean and straight.

Yet in practise, it doesn't work because something inside us knows it's wrong to achieve your own satisfaction by harming other people. That was Dostoyevsky's major theme from *Crime and Punishment* onward.

You can see why, like Dostoyevsky, I've always been fascinated by crime. It is the ultimate moral fable about what's wrong with human beings.

But what interests me so much is that I've started to learn how to create this effect by focused attention. In my autobiography, I cut out one important section for lack of space. I ended by throwing a whole chapter out of the book. I don't regret it, because much of it was discussion about sex, and I think there's probably enough sex in it.

What happened was, in 1988, I was on my way to London, en route to a publisher's conference in Northampton, and was feeling depressed because I seemed to have become impotent. Nothing is more dispiriting for the average male than to lose his ability to experience sexual arousal. It made me feel useless, so when I climbed on to the train at our local station I felt bored and irritable. But since I knew I had a nine-hour journey ahead of me, I decided to try and make use of it to try to induce some kind of inner pressure.

At first, I tried concentrating my attention on the passing scenery, but this had no effect. But then, at a station along the line, a crowd of schoolgirls got into the carriage, and provided a focus for attention. Their average age was, I imagine, about fourteen, and some had obviously graduated to bras. I proceeded to try and concentrate my attention through sexual fantasy, imagining being in a bedroom and unbuttoning blouses and unzipping skirts.

This exercise was not a great success, and by the time the girls got off the train in Plymouth I had still not succeeded in arousing the slightest sexual response. But after the school girls had all got off and I could see that I was actually starting to induce that glow of mental energy, I continued to push my mind again and again until I got to London. It had an effect of what I can only call 'energising my gaze', making everything I looked at intensely interesting. And it was like blowing a fire with bellows and watching the sparks fly and the flames begin to roar.

The interesting thing being that I could relax and forget it all for five minutes and then return to it, get the bellows going and there was the fire blazing away again. It didn't fade away.

Anyway, in London I had to change trains to go to Northampton. And I crossed from Paddington to King's Cross. I'd never travelled on this line before, and I received a pleasant surprise when I looked out of the window and saw that we were at Berkhamsted station. That was the place where Graham Greene had been at school, and where he'd played Russian roulette on Berkhamsted Common with his brother's revolver.

I'd often used that thought as a mental exercise to raise my concentration. And now I'd achieved that kind of intensity by deliberate long-term effort.

Well, when I got to the conference centre outside Northampton, I went to my room and realised I was finally beginning to feel tired. I went to the bar and had a large vodka martini to relax me. Then I went in to the big hall where they were giving us all dinner. It was an Elizabethan hall, very long and narrow, with a high pointed ceiling, and musicians' galleries. The hall itself wasn't much wider than this room. And of course with the big table right down the centre of the hall it meant that there wasn't really space between the backs of the chair and the walls. So once I was seated at the head of the table – being the guest of honour – I knew that I couldn't get out to go for a pee. Fortunately, the wine was really awful, so there wasn't any temptation to drink much. The food was just as bad – like our old school dinners. And the more I sat there the more I felt exhausted. Then, to my horror, I began to feel sick.

I could see there was no easy way of getting to the nearest lavatory. Behind me there was a window that led out on to the garden, and I decided that if the worst came to the worst I'd fling it open and vomit outside. But of course, that was the last thing I wanted to do – the guest of honour being sick out of the window.

Then as I sat there, I suddenly remembered the sense of control I'd been feeling all day. And as soon as I thought of that, the sickness vanished instantly. And back came the feeling of strength and energy. I'd put myself into another personality, so to speak. And there

I was glowing away again. And I went on to make an excellent speech, and ended the evening with a sense of achievement.

I had to travel back the next day, and I was looking forward to doing the same thing again. But it didn't work. My brain was shot. Like your leg muscles if you've done a long cycle ride.

But it shouldn't be so. Just as your calf muscles can get used to cycling, so your brain muscles can get used to concentrating. I didn't try to repeat the experience for a long time, believing I'd have to make an almighty effort lasting for hours. Then one day, driving to the supermarket, I did it again. And now I know the basic technique.

I've got a lawnmower that has a little pump primer attached to the carburettor. It's a kind of little bulb in a plastic pipe, and you keep squeezing it in and out until you get a feeling of resistance, which is the fuel flowing into the carburettor. And you have to do the same kind of thing to induce this inner pressure. If it doesn't work, leave it five minutes and try again. And the third or fourth time, you get that mental glow...

In the last chapter of my autobiography there's a reference to the Northampton train which doesn't make sense. I left it in accidentally, and asked my publisher to remove it when the paperback came out. But he's left it in.

BS: I'm not sure I noticed that.

CW: Good.

> [At this point, we leave for the hike with the dogs, one of which was almost whining at his feet. Later on, returning, I fire a few more

questions but realise I have all I need for the
story, and he was getting tired – not surpris-
ingly – as was I]

BS: How would you like to be seen and remembered and have your career looked at as a writer?

CW: I think I should probably be seen as the first of something or other. In the way, say, Freud is. The first optimistic philosopher in European history.

BS: Have people picked up on that?

CW: Not really, no. I mean since the autobiography has been out a few people have said this kind of thing. But it's never really been understood simply because my work has never really been understood.

BS: That I find bizarre and unfathomable. Although I suppose, in speaking to you I have told you that I have had personal experiences that I have felt have made it perfectly understandable to me. But I think one reason you have had the success you have had is your ability to communicate in simple language. This is one of the things I really like about your writing, is that there's hardly any Briticisms. I don't feel like I'm reading a British writer as it were – but I think that's probably just because it's good writing.

CW: I still use the word 'whom', when the rest of the world has changed it to 'who', I'm fucked if I'm going to change to 'who'.

BS: Was that a conscious effort on your part though, to… I suppose it's just simple… simplicity…

CW: Oh, no. When I was a child there was a magazine called Everybody's, in which there were all kinds of interesting articles on all kinds of interesting subjects.

I might find an article about HG Wells and his latest ideas on evolution. Or on the pre-Raphaelites and Dante Gabriel Rossetti and how they'd thrown his final poems into the grave with... with his wife, then he decided to publish them and dug her up.

So it was Everybody's that taught me to write. I loved its clear, straight communication. So when I set out to become a writer, I'd taught myself. And of course, I learned about writing clear prose from Bernard Shaw.

> [*Joy joins us in her chair, as I have shifted to the couch*]

BS: I haven't talked about the early days, but that was quite madness as well, wasn't it? With Joy's parents... the horsewhip...

CW: That's all in the book. There's not really anything to add to that. You know, it's quite interesting. I think I was extremely lucky to stumble across Joy because I could see immediately that she was intelligent and sweet natured. All writers have a natural craving to find embodiments of Goethe's Eternal Feminine, and I quickly realised that she was as close as I'd come. In Leicester, you see, girls who were intelligent were in extremely short supply. Probably in short demand too. So I was delighted to come across someone who was quite bright and had copies of Proust and Yeats and *Ulysses* on her shelf. [*He turns to Joy:*] Oh, by the way, the first edition of *Ulysses* has disappeared from your shed. Have you gone and put it somewhere for safety?

> [*It is eventually found, in the house*]

Article for 'The Big Idea'

During my teens, as an inveterate haunter of second-hand bookshops, I often saw copies of a book called *Sanine*, written in 1903 by a Russian writer named Mikhail Artsybashev. Very often it looked new, as if the former owner was glad to get rid of it. One day I bought it out of curiosity, and discovered that it was one of the most extraordinary novels I had ever read. The hero is a Russian student who shares the rebellious ideals of most of his generation. Vladimir Sanine is an attempt to create the ideal Russian hero – sane, balanced, intelligent, clear-sighted, totally unlike the neurotic heroes of Dostoyevsky.

In one typical scene he is in a boat with a girl who is attracted by him, and when she lets him kiss her, seizes his opportunity and, in spite of her resistance, takes her virginity.

The next day she is horrified at what has happened, and when he calls on her, tells him to go away. He begs her not to bear any ill will, and says that if she gives her fiancé as much happiness as she has given him, he will be a lucky man. Suddenly she decides to look on the bright side – after all, it is a beautiful day and they still find one another attractive. For a moment she sees the world as he sees it – as something simple and beautiful, which human beings spoil with their neurotic self-torments. They kiss 'like brother and sister', and when he has gone, she lies on the grass and reflects that some things are best forgotten.

Sanine exerted a tremendous influence on its generation, and although some of its ideas are simplistic, is still a delightful book to read.

I was reminded of *Sanine* when I came upon the ideas of one of the most remarkable of modern psychologists, Sydney Banks. He stumbled upon his central insight one day when he remarked to a friend: "I'm so unhappy." And the friend replied: "You're not unhappy Syd – you just think you are." The idea hit him like a revelation: that most human beings cause their own problems by their *thoughts*.

Although an ordinary working man, without a formal education, Banks was so stunned by this insight that he began giving lectures about it. Soon, he was giving seminars that were crowded with professional men – doctors, businessmen, psychiatrists.

A New York psychiatrist, George Pransky, who had begun to feel disillusioned about Freud, went along to a weekend seminar, and at first could not understand what Syd Banks meant when he said that all our problems are caused by our thoughts. But he observed that the people at the conference all seemed full of energy and optimism – that they were all 'copers' who were in charge of their lives. And when he grasped what Banks was saying, he suddenly began to share the feeling. He went on to apply these insights to his patients, and found that they worked. Pransky has created a psychology that is based on optimism about our capabilities.

The basic idea behind Pransky's 'psychology of mind' is simple. Our days are spent focusing on narrow horizons of awareness, a permanent state of 'close-up-ness', rather like going into a picture gallery and keeping your eyes two inches from the canvases. You would see the texture of the paint, but you would not see 'the picture'. Human beings are like this all the time. They are trapped in 'close-upness', in a worm's-eye view of reality. Their lives have an underpinning of boredom.

This vanishes the moment we are confronted by any kind of crisis. A man who was told he has an incurable disease would be rocketed out of the worm's-eye view into a bird's-eye-view, in which he is suddenly aware of the value of life. If, at that point, he learns that the doctors were mistaken and his life is in no danger, the relief would bring an interesting insight: that the bird's-eye view was true all along, and the worm's-eye view was a mistake caused by 'close-upness'. Now all he has to do is to tell himself beyond all possibility of doubt that the worm's-eye view is false and the bird's-eye view is true, and he has a means of transforming his life.

Hans Keller, former head of BBC music programmes,

once described how, in the 1930s, he was living in Germany and became aware that fellow Jews were vanishing into concentration camps. He said that he prayed: "O God, only let me get out of Germany, and I swear I'll never be unhappy again." Of course, he didn't succeed in living up to his promise. But it is easy for all of us to identify with that feeling that it would be quite easy to live up to it. And he had grasped the essence of Syd Banks's insight.

Now just over fifty years ago, I suddenly woke up to the same insight, and settled down to try and capture it in a book called *The Outsider*. Its starting point was the high number of artists and writers in the 19th Century who committed suicide. I could see that the basic problem was that they found the world of everyday life boring and discouraging. Yet every now and then, they would experience moments of immense happiness and intensity, in which the whole world became self-evidently glorious. The trouble was that when they woke up the next morning, the vision had evaporated, and the world seemed once again dull and dreary.

Clearly, what they needed was simply to grasp *intellectually*, as Syd Banks did, that the worm's-eye view was false.

It seemed clear to me that it was this damned 19th Century, with all its frustrated hopes, that was responsible for our neurotic civilisation, with its underlying pessimism. It is the 19th Century underpinning we have to get rid of.

As to who to blame for it, the answer seemed clear: the philosophers.

For example, in November 1811, the dramatist and

storywriter Heinrich von Kleist blew out his brains and those of his mistress because the philosophy of Kant had convinced him that life was meaningless and that the underlying reality is forever unattainable. Goethe's Faust had come to the same conclusion, and been on the point of suicide 'because we can nothing know' when the sound of the Easter bells caused his childhood to come flooding back and made him change his mind. But why should it matter if life is an illusion, so long as it is enjoyable? Because if it is an illusion, then free will is also an illusion, and we are merely machines. And that thought is enough to depress any sensitive soul. Descartes had argued that animals are machines, and in 1738 the French philosopher Julien de La Mettrie went one further in a book called *Man the Machine*, arguing that free will is an illusion. He was followed by a whole school of French thinkers like Condillac and Cabanis who argued that 'mental life' is merely a matter of physical sensations. Cabanis said the brain secretes thought as the liver secretes bile.

At which point, one of their school, Maine de Biran, had a revelation rather like Syd Banks's. He pointed out that whenever I make some real effort, I have a clear feeling that it is the 'I' who is doing this, and not a machine. But the French have always preferred pessimism to optimism, and Biran's insight was soon forgotten. And even now, two centuries later, psychology continues to insist that man is a machine, and that consciousness is a mere by-product of the brain.

But does it make any difference whether we are machines or not? Well yes, it does. If an intelligent person falls into depression, then the thought that he has no free will can push him over the edge, as it pushed Kleist.

An interesting new discovery in brain physiology underlines this. ECT, electroconvulsive therapy, was first used by Ugo Cerletti in the late 1930s. He discovered that if a current of about an amp is passed through the brain for half a minute, it is like a small version of an epileptic seizure, and it often cures depression. Johan Hellsten of Lund University now thinks he knows why. He tried giving rats ECT treatment, and found that it increased the number of epithelial cells – the cells that line blood vessels – in the part of the brain called the hippocampus. The vessels also increased their length by sixteen per cent. We know that long-term depressives have a smaller hippocampus than average, so curing it by ECT creates bigger and better cells.

Depression is a state in which we cease to use the will. And the muscles of the will suffer hypertrophy, just as the leg muscles of a bed-ridden patient waste will away. The shock of ECT seems to have the same effect as a sudden crisis, of stimulating us to effort. And willed effort causes something inside us to grow. So once George Pransky's patients have been taught to induce their own version of ECT by a combination of effort and optimism, they presumably begin to grow epithelial cells and turn into 'copers', suddenly finding they enjoy life.

All this is a striking justification for a theory of Nobel Prize winning brain physiologist, Roger Sperry, whose studies of the difference between our right and left cerebral hemispheres caused such a sensation in the 1960s.

Now, in traditional brain physiology, consciousness is regarded as a product of the brain, as heat is the product of a fire (or bile of the liver). As a traditional scientist, Sperry was willing to accept the proposition that consciousness is a product of the brain and cannot exist apart from it. But in a paper of 1980 called 'Mind-brain interaction: mentalism, yes; dualism, no', he shocked and upset his colleagues by announcing a view that struck them as pure heresy. He suggested that when we think and feel, consciousness operates on the brain as human fingers operate on a computer keyboard, or as an electric current operates on a television screen, making a picture out of 'dots'. Or, if you like, as the fingers of a pianist operate when he plays the piano. In other words, consciousness is not passive but active and 'creative'. Sperry had rediscovered Maine de Biran's free will.

Clearly there is one more step to take. And I suspect that if Sperry had not died in 1981 he would have taken it: to recognise that consciousness is not a mere product of the brain, but exists in its own right. A useful first move would be to persuade scientists like Johan Hellsten to begin experiments to try and show that brain cells can be created by a focused effort of will. That would lay the foundations for a new science, a new philosophy, and a new civilisation.

Introduction to Paul Hougham's
Gaia Atlas of Mind, Body and Spirit

The subject of this very remarkable work is one that has preoccupied me throughout my life – our hidden human potential.

From my first book *The Outsider* onward, I have been fascinated by those strange moments in which we experience a curious sense of power and happiness – what one philosopher called 'contact with the source of power, meaning and purpose'. It is rather like wandering along a familiar road, and finding a door in a wall that leads into some amazing garden – in fact, HG Wells created that image in his short story 'The Door in the Wall'.

Where is this magical door? The answer is quite clear: somewhere inside us. But why is it so hard to find, and how can we find our way back to it? This is the subject of the book you are now holding in your hands. It is a kind of atlas of our inner being.

This search for 'the door in the wall' has, of course, been known to every nation and culture on earth, and Paul Hougham is more qualified than most to talk about it, since he has an encyclopedic knowledge of world cultures.

I became interested in the problem of 'the door in the wall' as a child, for it presented itself to me every Christmas. There was a marvellous sense of inner peace, as if the world had made a truce and promised to smooth out all the difficulties of life. And as we walked down to my grandparents for tea, the streets I knew so well somehow looked different. And when Christmas was over, and 'reality' gradually returned, I found myself wondering, without putting it into words: Was that marvellous feeling an illusion? Or was it – as I felt strongly at the time – the 'real' reality behind the face of this difficult and often boring everyday life?

Here is an example that will underline my point, from a book called *Seeing the Invisible*, a collection of accounts of 'visionary' experiences submitted by ordinary people to the Alister Hardy Foundation:

> At the age of 22-23 I remember standing in my room when suddenly I felt 'dizzy' – overwhelmed by a sensation of 'light' – it felt as if flame was around me. It seemed as if I was transported on to another plane of consciousness, shot through with an almost unbearable joy.
>
> I don't know how long this experience lasted, maybe a few minutes or even

only a few seconds: it did not belong to a time-space world. The sensation of joy and inexplicable happiness lasted two or three days, gradually fading. It happened at a time in my life when I was enjoying things enormously in a normal way.

Now I cannot claim to have experienced the same kind of ecstasy. But I felt that the Christmas feeling, 'when I was enjoying things enormously', was a kind of prelude to it. And I suspect that every one of us could tell a similar story, for we all have a natural feeling that feelings of delight and intensity are somehow a natural human birthright.

Now as you will see from this book, many cultures have their own methods of approaching 'the door in the wall'. In fact, the Kaballah describes several different doors, each approached by a different path. Paul Hougham's chapter on it is one of the best short accounts I have read.

Now although I wrote a rather large book that included an account of the Kaballah – called *The Occult* – I have never given precedence to this approach. My own approach has always been psychological, and based upon the observation of the American psychologist Abraham Maslow, to the effect that *all* healthy people have, with a fair degree of frequency, what he called 'peak experiences' – experiences of sudden bubbling happiness, when we experience what GK Chesterton called 'absurd good news'.

Such experiences happen, of course, when we experience sudden relief from anxiety. And when we are oppressed with some worry, we have the feeling that *if only* this would go away, we would be able to feel happy for days or weeks.

Now for years I pursued my investigation into that question of the peak experience and how it comes about. And then, towards the end of 1979, I had a major breakthrough. This is how I describe it in a book called *The Devil's Party*:

> On New Year's Day, 1979, I was trapped by snow in a remote Devon farmhouse, where I had gone to lecture to extra-mural students. After 24 hours we decided we had to make an effort to escape. It so happened that my car was the only one that would climb the slope out of the farmyard. After several hours' hard work with shovels, we finally reached the main road.
>
> The snow on the narrow country road had been churned up by traffic, but was still treacherous. And in places where the snow was still untouched, it was hard to see where the road ended and the ditch began. So as I began to make my way home, I was forced to drive with total, obsessive attention. Finally back on the main Exeter road, where I was able to relax, I noticed that everything I looked at seemed curiously real and interesting. The hours of concentrated attention had somehow 'fixed' my consciousness in a

higher state of alertness. There was also an immense feeling of optimism, a conviction that most of our problems are due to vagueness, slackness, inattention, and that they are all perfectly easy to overcome with determined effort. This state lasted throughout the rest of the drive home. Even now, merely thinking about the experience is enough to bring back the insight and renew the certainty.

This experience of a 'more powerful' consciousness seemed a revelation, because it was not some sudden mystical 'flash'; *I had done it myself.* So it ought to be possible to do again.

I found it far more difficult than I had anticipated. I often tried it when driving, and achieved it briefly, but never for long. I did, in fact, succeed again on a long train journey. But when I tried again the next day, on the return journey, I found it impossible. Obviously, the effort had exhausted some inner energy. I began to suspect that it was the sense of emergency that had brought about my first success, and that this was difficult to create at will.

But over the years I have gone on trying. And finally, about two years ago, I found I was succeeding. I was succeeding in achieving the 'trick' that would achieve the kind of focused attention required to release this sense of access to some kind of brain-energy.

This focused attention brings with it an insight: that one of the byproducts of the quest for insight is our tendency for what might be called 'negative feedback'.

The author [Paul Hougham] puts his finger on the nature of the problem in his introduction, when he says:

> Ten years after Schrodinger's first meeting with his cat, the philosopher Maurice Merleau-Ponty published *The Phenomenology of Perception* in which he described for us greater possibilities of how we know things. Perception, he suggested, is neither the subjectivity of personal perception nor any objective reading of objects beyond our sphere, but rather a blended phenomenon of experience itself, constantly affecting itself. It is often argued that such qualities of subject contamination in the processes of perception occur only at a theoretical and quantum level of reality. But in each question we ask of the world, in the hypotheses of scientific experiment and our expectations as to what we see, we irrevocably shape what we find. This is the inter-subjective basis for every aspect of beingness within the universe. And as we will discover, we are powerful beings both at a global and personal level. What we seek we will find in the effects of our choices upon the health of our planet, our cultures, and our personal health and wellbeing.

It was when I was reading this passage that I suddenly

realised what an important book this is.

Another brilliant insight can be found in the epi-graph to the tenth chapter, 'We Don't Discover, We Create' – 'The neutrality of our participation in life is a merely limiting ruse; we inevitably create the texture of our lives.'

It is natural to see ourselves as passive because we spend so many years as children accepting that adults know what is going on, and what it is all about. Then we achieve adulthood, and discover that this was un-true. Adults don't know, any more than children do.

But some adults, just a few, understand. Merleau-Ponty understood, and he learned it from his master, the philosopher Edmund Husserl. He knew that per-ception is active, not passive – he called it 'intentional' – and that if we could learn to grasp that perception is an *unconsciously creative act*, we would have taken a vital step up the evolutionary ladder.

Phenomenology as a
Mystical Discipline

One evening early in 1933, Sartre and Simone de Beauvoir were having a drink with Raymond Aron, who had just returned from the French Institute in Berlin. Aron pointed to the apricot cocktail and said to Sartre: "You see, my dear fellow, if you were a phenomenologist, you could talk about this cocktail and make a philosophy out of it." Beauvoir says that Sartre 'turned pale with emotion', because this was what he had been longing to achieve for years – to describe objects just as he saw and touched them. Sartre immediately bought a book on Husserl, and began reading it as he walked home.

I experienced a similar insight in September 1961

during my first lecture tour of the United States. It lasted for three months, and I often visited several colleges or universities a week, talking non-stop for five or six hours a day. At every college I had to start again at the beginning, and summarise the ideas that I had developed in my first book *The Outsider*, and its sequels *Religion and the Rebel*, *The Age of Defeat* and *The Strength to Dream*.

Repeating my basic ideas over and over again made me familiar with them in a new way, and made me more aware of their implications. For example, I began to see that existentialism was simply a new form of 19th Century romanticism – Romanticism Mark II, so to speak. Romanticism Mark I was the 'eternal longing', that craving for something beyond mere material existence, which tormented so many 19th Century poets like a sickness. Most of the romantics concluded that it was unattainable, and sank into a despair that shortened their lives.

On the other hand, the existentialist philosophers, who had their roots in Kierkegaard, faced life with grim acceptance. In *The Myth of Sisyphus*, Camus says that Sisyphus is doomed to roll a rock uphill and watch it roll down again forever – yet we must consider Sisyphus happy, for he possesses the inner-freedom of his own mind. Sartre once remarked: "We are as free as you like, but helpless."

But Husserl's phenomenology had shown me the way out of the *cul de sac* of existentialism. Husserl's most basic idea, the intentionality of perception, means not only that we are free, but most emphatically *not* helpless.

Husserl had borrowed the idea of intentionality from his master Franz Brentano, who in *Psychology from an Empirical Standpoint* (1874) had defined psychology as the science of mental phenomena, which he distinguished from physical phenomena by saying that they 'intentionally include an object within themselves' – ie, I think *about* that table, that idea. Brentano's intentionality is 'about-ness'. But Husserl could see that intentionality is far more significant than mere 'aboutness'. He saw that *all perception is intentional.* If I do not fire my attention at something, I don't see it – or rather, I see it 'mechanically', hardly *noticing* it.

If perception is like an arrow fired at a target, then I must have a kind of 'inner-archer' who fires it. And if I can choose what I pay attention to, intentionality is an act of freedom. And if we can change our thoughts, we can change our lives, change the world.

More to the point, we can change our *inner* worlds.

Sartre and Camus had failed to recognise this. Sartre's most famous statement is: "Man is a useless passion." But how can we be useless if we are free?

The book I wrote as a consequence of these insights, *Beyond the Outsider*, begins by considering the fundamental human problem: whether, as Sartre and Camus insist, we have to accept that life is meaningless.

The case against life is summarised by Schopenhauer, who says that life is a pendulum that swings between misery and boredom. We experience some anxiety or inconvenience, strive to overcome it, feel momentary relief as it vanishes, then forget to feel relieved and relapse into boredom. And if this is true, then we had better accept 'unheroic nihilism' as the truth about the human condition: that life is bound to be unsatisfactory to an intelligent person because it is meaningless.

But in his *Experiment in Autobiography*, HG Wells had another explanation for the unsatisfactoriness. Men like himself, he says – 'originative intellectual workers' – find normal human existence boring because they long for a more meaningful kind of existence. "We are like early amphibians, so to speak, struggling out of the waters that have hitherto covered our kind, into the air, seeking to breathe in a new fashion and to emancipate ourselves from... necessities. At last it becomes a case of air or nothing. But the new land has not definitely emerged from the waters, and we swim distressfully in an element we wish to abandon."

In other words, we want a new *kind* of freedom than any animal has ever known.

In the chapter, 'The Strange Story of Modern Philosophy', I begin by considering the 'world rejection' of Socrates, who tells his followers that since the philosopher spends his life trying to separate his soul from his body, his own death should be regarded as a consummation. And this is consistent with his belief that only spirit is real, and matter is somehow unimportant and unreal. This notion would persist throughout the next two thousand years, harmonising comfortably with the Christian view that this world is unimportant compared to the next.

Then came scientific thought, in the person of Galileo, who introduced the spirit of experiment. He demonstrated that gravity makes all bodies fall at the same speed, and invented the telescope through which he discovered the moons of Jupiter. From then on, human thought began to take a more purposeful direction. In 1642, the year Galileo died, Newton was born, and within forty years, science had advanced further than in the previous two thousand.

In philosophy, a similar leap forward had taken place while Galileo was still alive. René Descartes attempted to bring into philosophy the same kind of certainty that Galileo had brought to science. Galileo had explored the heavens with a telescope; Descartes decided to examine the human situation through a kind of magnifying glass.

His new method of achieving certainty was simplicity itself: *to doubt everything*. After seeing some toy robots driven by water in the park at Versailles, it struck him that human beings are almost entirely mechanical; we need stimuli to make us do something. Of course, men could not be made of clockwork, because they have souls. (Descartes was a good Catholic.) But animals could be, and probably are, machines.

How do I know I am not a machine? Because a machine has no self-awareness. On the other hand, I can think, 'therefore I am'.

Such an assertion obviously leaves room for doubt. If some god could endow a washing machine with self-awareness, it would probably assume that it operates of its own free will, and would say 'I think, therefore I am'. It would clearly be mistaken.

The British philosopher John Locke – who was eighteen when Descartes died – recognised this. He did not actually argue that men are robots, but came very close to it when he said that we cannot know anything that does not come from our experience. There is nothing in the mind that was not first in the senses. When man is born, his mind is like a blank sheet of paper, a 'tabula rasa'. Everything he then learns arises from things that happen to him. So what we call the mind – all our thoughts, responses, reactions – is a 'construct', like a house built of pieces of Leggo.

Descartes had launched modern western philosophy with a dubious proposition, and now Locke continued it with an even more dubious one (for anybody who kept pigeons could have told Locke that they are born with all kinds of innate knowledge). This seems to be a typical characteristic of western philosophy: if someone makes a stupid howler, his successors try to justify it and carry the thing to even further lengths of absurdity, when common sense would suggest that they get their foundations right by going back to square one.

So it was perhaps inevitable that Bishop Berkeley should go a step further. If we can only know things through the mind, then why should we assume the outside world exists at all? Jam is not really sweet; it only produces a sensation of sweetness on the tongue. The sky is not really blue; it only produces a sense of blueness on the eyes. Perhaps objects only exist when we are looking at them, and when there is no one there to see them, they vanish. Or at least, they would if God was not there to see them.

This was obviously inviting some clever trouble-maker to suggest that, since there is no evidence that God exists, perhaps everything is an illusion? Which is more or less what the next 'great philosopher' did by carrying doubt even further. David Hume set out to reduce everything to materialism. The soul, which

Descartes thought he had proved, is an illusion, because when I look inside myself, I do not become aware of 'the essential me', but merely of thoughts and sensations. So human beings are also made of Lego.

And when you look at things in this piecemeal way, they simply dissolve. Even cause and effect are seen to be an illusion, for 'every effect is a distinct event from its cause', and therefore 'cannot be discovered in the cause'. Perhaps God is pulling our legs when He makes a kettle boil on a fire; perhaps it is really supposed to freeze.

What Hume did was to sweep the world bare of all certainty, leaving philosophy looking like a landscape after the dropping of an H-bomb.

The philosopher who tried to repair the damage was the Königsburg professor Immanuel Kant. And what he did was, in effect, to take a step backward to Bishop Berkeley, and make the mind the creator of reality.

He noticed the existence of what Husserl would later called 'intentionality' – that the mind makes sense of this chaotic world that surrounds us by imposing order on it. We divide things into categories – for example, everything I can see around me is either a liquid, a solid or a gas. We use clocks to impose order on the chaos of time, and measuring rods to impose it on space. We call things by words we have invented – that four legged creature is a 'cat', and that one a 'dog'. You could say we invent space and time to make our world orderly enough to live in comfortably. It is as if we had invented a pair of spectacles that impose categories on the world.

Does that mean there is no 'true reality' behind all

our categories? Yes, there *is* such an underlying reality, which Kant called the noumena, to distinguish it from the world of mere 'phenomena' that surrounds us. But since we can never remove the spectacles, we can never know this reality.

At which point one of Kant's followers, a now almost forgotten thinker called Johann Gottlieb Fichte, called a halt to the madness – at least, he would have done if anyone had taken any notice of him. What Fichte said was: Why bother about this 'noumena'? If it is unknowable, we may as well forget it. In that case, man is left in a world created by his senses – just as Berkeley said. But if 'I' really created the universe, why do I not *know* that I did? There must be two 'me's', this everyday self who has no idea of what is going on, and another 'me' who is actually a kind of god who has created this world.

Descartes sat in his armchair, or more likely lay in bed (he was notoriously lazy) and asked: What can I know for certain? He answered: Two things are certain – my own existence and that world out there. We call them the subjective and the objective worlds. Fichte said: No, there are *three* worlds – that world out there, and two 'me's', the ordinary me and the me who is behind the scenes creating the world out there.

The next question is: how could the ordinary 'me' begin to explore the extraordinary world created by the 'other me'? And this, of course, is the true task of phenomenology, to which we shall come in a moment.

Fichte made one more comment that is of immense importance: that the trouble with philosophy was that its attitude to the world is *passive*. But philosophy, he said (in *Addresses to the German Nation*) should regard itself as active, or at least as a prelude to action.

Expressed in this way, this sounds unexciting – as if it is merely an earlier statement of Karl Marx's remark that the business of philosophy is not to understand the world but to change it. In fact, it was really a blinding flash of insight: that Kantian philosophy turned philosophers into armchair theorists, so that their whole *attitude* to knowledge was passive, when to really grasp reality it should be active.

As to that other problem, that philosophical hare set running by Descartes, the solution seems to lie in Fichte's insight that we have 'two selves'.

Descartes should have followed up his assertion 'I think therefore I am' with 'Yes, but who am I?' He is failing to question *his own identity*, and this error will lead on to the errors of Locke, Berkeley, Hume, Kant, Hegel and the rest.

Husserl's phenomenology was an attempt to get back to square one to sort out the mess. But at about the same time, another thinker, Alfred North Whitehead, was doing this independently.

Whitehead began by returning to Hume, and pinning down the underlying fallacy. Hume argued that we have no true 'inner self'. He claimed that when he looked inside himself for 'the real David Hume', he only came across ideas and impressions, but nothing like a 'self'. And he concluded that all that can be found inside us is a 'stream of consciousness', a lot of scurrying thoughts whose only 'identity' is that they come one after another. This is the realisation that comes, he says, when you look at your inner self through a magnifying glass.

In a little book called *Symbolism, Its Meaning and Effect*, Whitehead points out that this method of looking at something through a magnifying glass is a good way of missing its meaning. If, for example, you looked at a great painting through a magnifying glass, you would only see the texture of the paint. If you look at a newspaper photograph close-up, you would only see disconnected dots. In both cases you are looking at individual trees and failing to see that they constitute a wood. In order to see the wood, we need to take a *bird's-eye view*, to stand back.

So we have two kinds of perception: bird's-eye and worm's-eye, close-up and far-off. Both only give half the truth.

Whitehead calls these two modes 'presentational immediacy' and 'causal efficacy'. The first is easy to understand – what is in front of your nose. The second is more difficult. The example Whitehead gives is the words 'United States'. You do not grasp these piecemeal: "United – that means held together. States – yes, that means states like Florida and California. Oh yes, that mean's America..." You see the two words as one, United States, and register that as 'America'. Cause and effect blend into one.

Now Hume criticised causality by saying that every effect is quite distinct from its cause, and so is not 'necessarily' linked to it. Whitehead replies: When you grasp a *'meaning'* cause and effect are not merely linked – *they are one.*

We might say, then, that we have two 'modes of perception', which could be called 'immediacy perception' and 'meaning perception'. When you are very tired and depressed, your meaning-perception becomes blurred (Sartre calls it nausea; the world dissolves into bits and pieces). But this is an illusion, caused by tiredness. On the other hand, when you are drunk and feeling jolly, the world seems to be *all* meaning. Then it is your immediacy perception that becomes blurred; you cannot even get your key into the keyhole.

On the other hand, there are times – perhaps when you are feeling happy and excited on a spring morning – when the two modes of perception seem to blend together perfectly. You have a wonderful sense of meaning, yet your 'immediacy perception' is fully operational.

What happens then could be compared to the film *The Dam Busters*, in which the British planes had to drop bombs shaped like billiard balls that bounced along the Moener Lake and hit the dam at water level. The problem for the pilot was to know when he was at exactly the right height to drop them. The solution was to place two spotlights on the plane, one in the nose, one in the tail, whose two beams converged at exactly the right height. So when there was just one spot on the surface of the lake, he released the bombs.

According to Whitehead, our most brilliant moments of insight happen when the two beams – 'immediacy perception' and 'meaning perception' – converge.

This, then, is Whitehead's 'refutation of Hume', and it is a breakthrough in western philosophy because it provides new foundations. The question 'Do we have free will or are we robots?' becomes absurd. Instead, philosophy can get back to its proper business – 'understanding the universe'.

And what of that other question: of the 'me' behind the scenes, whose existence was recognised by Fichte?

This was the problem to which Edmund Husserl devoted his life.

When he was at university, in the 1880s, philosophy was still struggling to throw off the toils of Bishop Berkeley, and the notion that 'meaning' is something created by the mind. John Stuart Mill, for example, argued that the feeling of logical certainty is no more than that – a feeling – and that all logic can be therefore reduced to psychology. This notion is called 'psychologism', and in its broadest sense it holds that philosophy, logic – even mathematics – can be explained in terms of psychology. This outraged Husserl, for it implied that all truth is 'relative', and Husserl could see that philosophy is never going to escape from muddle and confusion while it accepted such vagaries. So his starting point was the acceptance that logic deals with objective truth, not with relative ideas.

His first major work, *Logical Investigations*, was a sustained attack on psychologism, and an attempt to show that philosophy should be nothing less than a *science*.

This, of course, is what Descartes wanted to do when he asked the question: 'Of what can we be certain?' Husserl gave Descartes full credit for this, and even entitled one of his most important series of lectures *Cartesian Meditations*. But, as we have seen, Descartes's problem was that he began with the wrong question: 'What can I know?', failing to ask who was this 'I' who wanted to know.

Let me try putting this another way. In her book about 'female outsiders' *Alone, Alone*, Rosemary Dinnage discusses Bertrand Russell's affair with Ottoline Morrell, and says: "It is important to understand… that it was his underlying need to know whether anything could be established as true that shaped his whole mind… He himself felt that his search had made him into a 'logic machine', a 'spectator and not an actor', with a 'mind like a search light, very bright in one direction but dark everywhere else'."

What Russell had recognised was what Fichte had said a century earlier: that real philosophy demands an *active* attitude, rather than the passive one of the philosopher sitting in his armchair. To 'know' something merely with the mind is hardly to know it at all. Our whole being is somehow involved in true knowing. And when this happens, knowledge has a 'weight' that is not found in merely intellectual knowing.

And this is also the essence of Husserl's revolution: that consciousness is intentional, that it is active, not passive. It is like a hand reaching out and grabbing things, not just a searchlight. And Russell's own career is a sad example of what happens when a thinker stays in the 'Cartesian' attitude to philosophy. Russell spent his whole life asking: 'What can we know for certain?' And the result is oddly disappointing, for he never found a satisfactory answer.

But if, like Rosemary Dinnage, we remove our attention from Russell the thinker to Russell the person, we become aware of the consequences of his 'passive' attitude to philosophy – that is, he totally failed to bring his interior philosopher and human being into line. As his second wife Dora put it to Rosemary Dinnage: "Bertie could behave *rottenly*." Until he was a very elderly gentleman he continued to pursue women, and to behave like an adolescent. As a person, he remained deeply unsatisfying to all the women he got involved with, and was dumped innumerable times. (I imagine his lifelong desire to screw any attractive female, from fifteen to fifty, was due to a gloomy conviction in adolescence that a person so ugly and preoccupied with ideas would remain love-starved, and by the time he learned different, the neurosis was too deep to be unrooted.)

But how could a person like Russell have benefited from Husserl's phenomenology? In fact, we may as well open the question out and ask: How could *anyone*?

Let me start by quoting the French phenomenologist Paul Ricoeur. He is talking about the 'reduction' or *epoché*, that method of 'standing back' and viewing things from a distance – rather like standing back from a large picture in an art gallery:

> By means of this reduction conscious-
> ness rids itself of a naiveté which it has
> beforehand, and which Husserl calls the
> natural attitude. This attitude consists in
> spontaneously believing that the world
> which is there is simply given. In correct-
> ing itself about this naiveté, consciousness
> discovers that it is in itself giving, sense-
> giving. The reduction does not exclude
> the presence of the world; it takes nothing
> back. It does not even suspend the prima-
> cy of intuition in every cognition. After
> the reduction, consciousness continues

seeing, but without being absorbed in this seeing, without being lost in it. Rather, the very seeing itself is discovered as a *doing* (*opération*), as a producing (*oeuvre*) – once Husserl even says "as a creating". Husserl would be understood – and the one who thus understands him would be a phenomenologist – if the intentionality which culminates in seeing were recognised to be a creative vision. (*Husserl. An Analysis of his Phenomenology*, 1987)

But *how?*, the reader wants to ask. What is the trick of transforming ordinary perception into creative vision?

We can begin by noting that poets do it all the time, so do great painters like Van Gogh. Read Shelley's 'Ode to the West Wind', and you can feel the 'phenomenological vision'. Or look at a great painting by Van Gogh or Vlaminck or Soutine. When I was working in a tax office in Rugby in my teens, I remember my boss saying with disgust that he thought Van Gogh simply distorted everything he painted. He was missing the point: that Van Gogh was saying: '*This* is how I see things when I put on my creative spectacles.' Rupert Brooke said that on a spring morning he sometimes walked down a country road feeling almost sick with excitement.

Brooke realised that he could bring on this feeling by looking at things in a certain way. And what was really happening when he did this was that he had somehow become aware that he could *see more*, become aware of more, by looking at things as if they possessed hidden depths of meaning. *For it is true.* He was becoming conscious of the intentional element in perception, that his 'seeing' was in itself a creative act.

We can suddenly begin to see what Ricoeur meant. Let me try putting this another way.

A normal young male feels spontaneous sexual excitement if he sees a girl taking off her clothes. He feels this is 'natural', like feeling hungry when you smell cooking. But supposing he is looking through an art book with reproductions of paintings, and he sees a picture of a model taking off her clothes. She is attractive, and he stares at the painting, and then – let us suppose – deliberately induces sexual excitement. How does he do this? In that question lies the essence of phenomenology. You could say that he looks at the picture, and deliberately puts himself in the state of mind of a man about to climb into bed with her. He ceases to see the picture from 'the natural standpoint' ("this is just a picture") and deliberately endows it with a dimension of reality. And it can be seen that he is again 'putting on his creative spectacles'. In fact, as Derrida has pointed out, the act of masturbation is a textbook illustration of intentionality in action.

The mind can deliberately *change* the way it sees things. Brooke tells how he can wander about a village wild with exhilaration: "And it's not only beauty and beautiful things. In a flicker of sunlight on a blank wall, or a reach of muddy pavement, or smoke from an engine at night, there's a sudden significance and importance and inspiration that makes the breath stop with a gulp of certainty and happiness. It's not that the wall or the smoke seem important for anything or suddenly reveal any general statement, or are suddenly seen to be good or beautiful in themselves – only that *for you* they're perfect and unique. It's like being in love with a person... I suppose my occupation is being in love with the universe."

We can grasp what Ricoeur meant by 'the very seeing is discovered as a *doing*'. Brooke is so excited because he realises he can *make himself* see things in a certain way, and respond to them – just as an adolescent is excited when he discovers that this body can produce a heady brew called sexual excitement. And this is the very essence of phenomenology: you might say that phenomenology is a prosaic way of developing the mystical faculty.

Appendix 1*

Let us, simply as an exercise, see if we can recognise the most fundamental of these levels. Let us start off with the basic state of non-consciousness that we experience in very deep sleep, and call this Level Nought. In that case Level One is the level we experience as we dream, and which persists in hypnologic experiences.

Level Two is the most basic level of waking consciousness: that is, mere awareness. A child experiences this when he is too tired to take any interest in anything. He may be on his way home from a party but he gazes blankly at the passing world. If you were to ask, "What have you just seen?" he would reply, "I don't know." His consciousness is merely a mirror reflecting the outside world. Nietzsche once said that we envy the cows their placidity, but it would be no use asking them the secret

* 'The Seven Levels of Consciousness', from *Beyond the Occult* pp347-348, Carroll & Graf, 1988

of their happiness for they would have forgotten the question before they could give the answer. This is Level Two.

At Level Three, consciousness has become self-aware but it is still dull and heavy – so heavy that we are only aware of one thing at a time: everything seems to be merely itself, utterly without meaning, and your own reflection in a mirror seems to be a stranger. This is the level that Sartre calls nausea.

Level Four is the normal consciousness we experience every day. It is no longer too heavy to move: it has learned how to cope with existence yet it tends to think of life as a grim battle – possibly a losing battle. Consequently, it tends to sink back easily towards Level Three and to find experience meaningless and boring.

So far the one thing the levels all have in common is a basically passive attitude towards life and experience. At Level Five this ceases to be so. This is a level that I have labelled provisionally 'spring morning consciousness' or 'holiday consciousness'. It is characterised by that bubbling feeling of happiness we experience when life suddenly becomes more interesting and exciting and all kinds of prospects seem to be opening up in front of us. Quite suddenly caution and doubt disappear; life becomes self-evidently fascinating and delightful. This is the feeling that Hesse's Steppenwolf experiences as he tastes a glass of wine and is reminded of 'Mozart and the stars'.

Level Six could be labelled the 'magical level'. It is what happens to a child on Christmas Day, when everything combines to make life seem wonderful. Or imagine the consciousness of two honeymooners on their wedding night looking down from a balcony on to a moonlit lake, with the dark shapes of mountains in the distance. In such states we feel a total reconciliation with our lives. "For moments together my heart stood still between delight and sorrow to find how rich was the gallery of my life," says Steppenwolf. Problems seem trivial; we see that the one real virtue is courage. Consciousness has become a continuous mild peak experience, what JB Priestley calls 'delight'"

Level Seven is Faculty X – Toynbee's experience on Pharsalus, Proust's experience as he tastes the madeleine dipped in tea. There is an almost godlike sensation: "I had ceased to feel mediocre, accidental, mortal…" This is more than a peak experience: it is an odd sense of mastery over time, as if every moment of your life could be recalled as clearly as the last ten minutes. We suddenly realise that time is a manifestation of the heaviness of the body and the feebleness of the spirit. We can also see that if we could learn to achieve this condition of control permanently, time would become, in a basic sense, non-existent.

The most interesting thing about the levels beyond Level Seven – the levels explored by Ouspensky and other mystics – is that they seem to contradict the evidence of our senses and of everyday consciousness. The inner becomes the outer, the outer becomes the inner, man is the whole universe and a mere atom, space and time are seen to be illusions and so on. Yet we can see that these contradictions are already inherent in everyday consciousness. At Level Two consciousness has no kind of 'connectedness'; it is merely a flow of meaningless impressions. Level Three – nausea – starts to arrest this flow, to connect things together, but it keeps collapsing into a sudden perception that the world is after all quite meaningless and futile. Level Four – ordinary consciousness – 'connects' things to a far higher degree, yet it still takes it for granted that life is an endless uphill struggle and that we have to make a continuous effort to see any meaning in it. At Level Five – 'holiday consciousness' – all this changes: there is a sense of being able to see to distant horizons, of becoming aware of 'Mozart and the stars'. We suddenly realise that the world around us is so fascinating in itself that no effort is required. Everything makes us think of something else and so we are kept in a continuous state of interest and excitement.

At Level Six – 'magic consciousness' – we seem to be floating in a sea of meaning and find it hard to understand how we could ever have been unhappy, or how anyone else could be. Even the worst experiences of the past now seem deeply interesting attempts to teach us something, essential steps on the upward path to this sense of optimism and control. The only tragedy in the universe seems to be that so many people lack the courage and sheer dogged stubbornness to keep going and so miss this literally 'heavenly' sense of wonder and reconciliation. Level Seven, with its sense of freedom, of mastery over time, is only a short step from the mystical level, just as Level Six – 'magic'– is only a short step from Faculty X. A sudden additional effort can carry the mind over the threshold into that strange realm where 'separateness' is seen to be a delusion caused by fatigue and everything is seen to be connected. One of the most encouraging things about this insight into the levels is that each level is only a short and easy step away from the previous one.

About the Authors

Colin Wilson was born in Leicester, England, in 1931 into a working-class background. He is the author of a hundred books, with subjects ranging from existential philosophy, psychology and criminology to the paranormal, fiction and plays. His first book, *The Outsider*, appeared in 1956 and was almost unanimously hailed by reviewers as a master-piece. His other publications include *Ritual in the Dark*, *The Strength to Dream*, *The Occult*, *The Misfits: a Study of Sexual Outsiders*, *From Atlantis to the Sphinx*, *A Criminal History of Mankind* and his autobiography, *Dreaming to Some Purpose*. He lives in Gorran Haven, near St Austell, Cornwall, with his wife, Joy.

Brad Spurgeon, a Canadian, has worked at the International Herald Tribune in Paris since 1983. In addition to reporting regularly about Formula One motor racing for that newspaper and The New York Times, he has written on a variety of subjects – from crime fiction to medicine to chess – for the IHT and other newspapers and magazines around the world. He has also published several short stories.